50 BADASS
Cat Ladies
WHO ROCKED THE WORLD

Written by:
Tilly

Illustrated by:
Emily Skinner

'Recently, embracing your inner cat lady has become not only acceptable, it's even fashionable [...] our current cat lady era could be seen as a feminist win.'

Lauren Cochrane, *Elle* magazine online,
6th of Feb 2024

INTRODUCTION

It seems that the 'Crazy Cat Lady' from the Simpsons is long over and done with. Now, being called a 'Cat Lady' is cool.

In 2021, JD Vance didn't know the major role he was about to play in debunking the crazy cat lady myth when he unashamedly called the Democrats' leaders, namely Kamala Harris, "a bunch of childless cat ladies who are miserable at their own lives" during a televised interview.

His infamous slur became viral during the American presidential elections in 2024, when he was chosen by Trump as VP candidate for the Republicans.

Cat lady pride invaded social media and brought an unprecedented scratch of feline feminism to the sign of the times. Taylor Swift gave the new term and the associated meme its rightful crown in her social media endorsement of Kamala Harris, signing "Taylor Swift, Childless Cat Lady."

The crazy cat lady myth dates back to the Middle Ages, where single women living with hordes of cats and not following societal norms were deemed complicit of the devil. But before cats were associated with Satan by the Roman Catholic Church, they were glorified in other cultures to the level of deities. For ancient Egyptians, the half-woman half-cat deity Bastet was the goddess of domesticity, childbirth, and 'women's secrets'. In China, Li Shou was a cat goddess and a symbol of fertility. Freyja, in Norse mythology, who rode a chariot led by cats, was the goddess of strength and beauty.

This book celebrates 50 badass women through the centuries to the present day, who rocked the world with their pioneering character and look on life, while celebrating the strongest bond with the most mysterious and independent pet species, the almighty cat.

From Egyptian Queen Nefertiti to Chinese poet Li Qingzhao, astrophysicist Margherita Hack, actress Audrey Hepburn and of course pop icon Taylor Swift, these illustrious women have significantly marked their times, but first and foremost, they were cat lovers. Perhaps even... cats themselves? In their souls at least, after all, doesn't a cat have nine lives?

Fiercely independent, strong-minded, elegantly mysterious and most of all, untamed – what could be a better compliment than 'cat lady'?

CONTENTS

Kamala Harris

Enya

Lauren Bacall

Magdaleine Pinceloup De La Grange

Eartha Kitt

ALICE WALKER

BORN IN GEORGIA, USA IN 1944

"Alice Walker contains multitudes. She is a truth-telling, word-working, change-conjuring, culture-shifting, revolutionary artist and citizen of the world."

Tayari Jones, New York Times bestselling author of *An American Marriage*

Alice Walker revolutionised literature as a Black woman writer in her endeavours to decolonise the minds.

She has a deep connection with her ancestors and always positions herself as a being within nature. When describing the creative process of her Pulitzer Prize-winning novel *The Color Purple*, she placed that relationship with nature and ancestral history as key. In that respect, she also relates with First Nation cultures.

Throughout her life, she has been an advocate for cat rescue and celebrated her close relationship with cats. Tuscaloosa, a cat who came into Walker's life soon after her divorce, would sit on her feet or lap while she wrote. She named another cat after Frida Kahlo in the hopes that "despite her horrendous kittenhood, she would, like Kahlo, develop into a being of courage, passion, and poise." She once said about a snaggle toothed rescue: "A stranger might look at her and say, 'Oh, she has imperfect teeth.' But I look at her and see the absolute perfection — the charming perfection — of her imperfection."

GROUND BREAKING FACTS ABOUT ALICE WALKER

Civil rights activist in the early 1960s, marching in Washington with Martin Luther King, Jr

First legal interracial married couple living in Mississippi (1968)

First African American woman to win the Pulitzer Prize for fiction in 1982 for *The Color Purple*

First Black, queer, feminist novel to achieve commercial and critical success: *The Color Purple*

Steven Spielberg adapted *The Color Purple* into a movie (1985)

Adaptation of *The Color Purple* into a Broadway musical (2005)

Adaptation of *The Color Purple* into a film musical (2023)

A 'Womanist': a term first coined by Alice Walker in her 1983 book *In Search of Our Mothers' Gardens*. It defines a Black feminist or feminist of colour, encapsulating values of a Black woman's strength, audacity, love for herself, other women, and all of humanity

In 2022, 500 pages of her journals, spanning four decades, were published under the title *Gathering Blossoms Under Fire: The Journals of Alice Walker*

Alice Walker has sold more than 15 million copies of her books, translated in over two dozen languages.

ALICE WALKER STAGED A WEDDING CEREMONY WITH HER CAT AND HER DOG IN 2006 BECAUSE, SHE SAID, SHE WANTED TO HONOUR HER CONNECTION TO THE ANIMALS.

ANITA EKBERG

BORN IN MALMÖ, SWEDEN IN 1931;
DIED IN ROCCA DI PAPA, ITALY IN 2015

Anita Ekberg was a Swedish actress immortalised in Fellini's 1960 masterpiece *La Dolce Vita*, where she was filmed wading through the Trevi Fountain, in the middle of the night, wearing a glamorous low-cut black dress. The scene was perceived as scandalous and the Vatican condemned it at the time.

But for cat lovers, the preceding scene when Sylvia (played by Anita Ekberg) finds a white kitten lost in the street, is much more iconic. She insists they find milk for the kitten although Rome is shut and empty in the late hours of the night. While her night companion, the news reporter played by Marcello Mastroianni makes arrangements to find milk, she wanders in the streets with the kitten and eventually puts it on her head. This scene undeniably established her as the 'sex kitten goddess' of all cinema times and the ultimate 'cat lady on screen' (together with Audrey Hepburn in *Breakfast at Tiffany's*).

IN HIS 1953 SONG "I SHALL BE FREE", BOB DYLAN WROTE THAT "BRIGITTE BARDOT, ANITA EKBERG AND SOFIA LOREN" WAS WHAT THE US NEEDED AS A COUNTRY "TO GROW".

> *"The luminous colour of her skin, her clear ice-blue eyes, golden hair and exuberance, joie de vivre made her into a grandiose creature, extraterrestrial and at the same time moving and irresistible."*
>
> **Fellini**

La Dolce Vita was her breakthrough in cinema, after having been elected Miss Sweden at the age of twenty and having had a few roles in Hollywood, such as Henry Fonda's adulterous wife in *War and Peace* (1956). Anita Ekberg had a strong sense of her beauty and her identity, although she was quite shy. When Hollywood producers asked her to change her nose as well as her name, she utterly refused even though she was just a 'starlet' at the time. Her confident and direct attitude led to the Hollywood world calling her 'Ekberg the Iceberg'. Nevertheless, Marcello Mastroianni warmed up to her on set and

they shared great chemistry on screen.

Anita Ekberg retired in 2002 after 50 years in the motion picture industry. Sadly, she didn't turn to cats as companions in her elderly life, but overpowering Great Danes instead, who caused her to have a hip injury. She had two unhappy marriages with alcoholic husbands, and the end of her life was quite tragic after a burglary in her villa, which left her in financial hardship. If only she had had a beautiful cat to comfort her, stand by her like an Egyptian god, shining in the gold sunrays, looking straight to the horizon, like a guardian of her timeless beauty.

ANTONELLA BOTTAZZI

BORN IN PIEMONTE, ITALY IN 1944;
DIED IN ITALY, IN 1997

"This shyness of mine prevents me from having 'open' communication with those close to me. Instead, with songs, I become aggressive."

First Italian female singer-song writer, Antonella Bottazzi was discovered in the mid-sixties on a music contest television programme.

She could almost be considered as the Italian Joan Baez. Tall with long brown hair, elegant, slender, wearing cat eye makeup. A true free spirit and defender of feminism and anti-consumerism.

Oracle.net tells us that the meaning of Antonella is 'priceless'/'praiseworthy'. And she was! But so little seems to have been written and archived about her pioneering career.

A beautiful photo shoot of her wearing vintage clothes, posing with a kitten, was done in 1972 in Milan. Those iconic pictures are one of the scarce testimonies to her modernity and femininity for that time in Italy.

When interviewed for the newspaper *Il Corriere della Sera* that same year, she said:

"I haven't worn a bra for two years. It's a way like another for me to feel freer. Let's not call it a 'protest'. It's too loaded and over-used a term. Let's just acknowledge that I'm in love with simplicity. That's all."

Nevertheless, she was perceived as a voice for feminism in the 1960s and 1970s Italy.

'Rebellious' and 'Anti-conformist' were recurring labels in the press to describe her personality.

Antonella Bottazzi was natural, authentic, and loved animals. Unsurprisingly, she dedicated the B side to her third EP *Il Ragazzo di Spagna* (1969) to ... "*Un gatto!*" (... "*A Cat!*")

The song starts with the following lyrics:

**'In un mondo di cane, come potre
Sopravivere un gatto...come potre ?
[...]
Ogni gatto sa vedere anche al buio'**

**('In a dog's world, how could a cat survive...
how could it?
[...]
Every cat can see in the dark')**

This song has more of a rock sound than her other songs, which are closer to light melodies ('melodie leggere') and ballads. She had a beautiful, pure and powerful low voice, full of character.

She was also a romantic. When interviewed about her first album, she said:

"It's my megalomania's fault. I like to talk about myself and always be at the centre of the stories I write. Even when they are stories told to me by others."

The album cover was provocative, featuring a small doll slayed in the belly by a kitchen knife.

HER SECOND AND LAST ALBUM IN 1979 WAS ONE FOR CHILDREN, CENTRED AROUND ANIMAL THEMES, STILL CELEBRATED TODAY.

AUDREY HEPBURN

BORN IN BRUSSELS, BELGIUM IN 1929;
DIED IN SWITZERLAND, IN 1993

"I believe in pink. I believe that laughing is the best calorie burner. I believe in kissing, kissing a lot. I believe in being strong when everything seems to be going wrong. I believe that happy girls are the prettiest girls. I believe that tomorrow is another day, and I believe in miracles."

Audrey Hepburn

Audrey Hepburn was born in Brussels in 1929 and went to school in Great Britain (her mother was a Victorian aristocrat). Her dad abandoned them when she was only six years old. They had unfortunately moved to Holland just before World War II broke out. Although Audrey was just a teenager, she performed as a young ballerina to raise money for the Resistance against German Nazi occupation. She also handed out secret messages. This period marked her terribly with the loss of two of her uncles.

AFTER THE WAR, AUDREY DREAMED OF BECOMING A PROFESSIONAL BALLET DANCER, BUT SHE WAS TOO TALL AND STARTED WITH SMALL ACTING ROLES INSTEAD.

She was propelled to Hollywood fame after her leading role with Gregory Peck in *Roman Holiday* in 1953. Her signature role as Holly Golightly in *Breakfast at Tiffany's* (1961) established her as a timeless style icon, wearing the famous Givenchy 'Little Black Dress'.

As an animal lover, bringing her dogs on sets, she hated the scene in *Breakfast at Tiffany's* when she had to toss the cat out of the cab. When she desperately tries to find it under the rain, Orangey, whom she calls 'Cat' throughout the movie, reappears desolate in a small crate. She bursts into tears and picks it up as she sees her protagonist Paul Varjak waiting for her. In this romantic scene, Orangey may symbolise love and attachment, but also the conflict that they might represent at times...

TOP AWARDS AND HONORS:

Academy Award (Oscar):
Best Actress in a Leading Role for *Roman Holiday* (1954)

Tony Award:
Best Actress in a Play (1954) for her performance in *Ondine*

BAFTA Awards:
Won three times for Best British Actress (in 1954 for *Roman Holiday*; in 1960 for the *The Nun's Story*; in 1963 for *Charade*)

Lifetime Achievement Awards:
Received in 1992 the BAFTA Special Award and the Golden Globe Award

Humanitarian Awards:
Received the Presidential Medal of Freedom in 1992 and other awards for her work as Goodwill Ambassador with UNICEF

AUDREY HEPBURN WAS REVERED FOR HER TALENT, HER GRACE, HER ELEGANCE, HER CHARM AND SENSE OF HUMOUR. CELEBRATED BY HER PEERS AS 'A COMPLETE CLASS ACT'.

BETTY WHITE

BORN NEAR CHICAGO, USA IN 1922;
DIED IN LOS ANGELES, USA IN 2021

Betty White, frequently hailed as the 'First Lady of television', had a television career in America spanning 80 years. It is no surprise that she claimed the Guinness World Record for the longest TV career as a female entertainer.

Her ditzy and 'terminally naïve' character in *The Golden Girls* won the hearts of American viewers for 180 episodes, during seven years. Betty White was truly loved as a TV and entertainment legend. She would deliver bawdy jokes in the softest manner and smile, and continued to appear in sitcoms even in her late eighties. No wonder she was called 'America's grandmother'.

All her life, she was an advocate for animals, loving wildlife and the outdoors.

"Animals don't lie, they don't criticize and if they have moody days, they handle it better than most humans do"

Betty White

She joined the Greater Los Angeles Zoo Association board of trustees in 1974 and in a recent National Geographic documentary, she was filmed soothing a lion, when the rest of the crew were terrified.

At home, Betty had several cats including a Himalayan named Mr. Bob, who lived with her for 11 years after he 'found her' and stayed.

Betty was 'young' in attitude and embodied in a certain manner the aspiring 'wellderly'. *The New Yorker* celebrated *The Golden Girls* as "a senior subculture, with its own fashion, politics, and humor." It was a coup at the time that the show writer Susan Harris managed to convince the board of the TV network to run a sitcom with women in their fifties and sixties as the main stars. Betty Friedan, a leading feminist voice, applauded the show for breaking "universal grayout of older women on network TV." For six of its seven seasons, it held the top spot in the ten most-watched shows.

One of Betty White's last roles was the voice of a tiger, Bitey White, in the 2019 animated film, *Toy Story 4*.

First award: a regional Emmy for outstanding personality in Los Angeles (1952)

First American woman to present a talk show solo with *Hollywood on Television* that ran live for five and a half hours a day, six days a week

Won 2 Emmys for her role as Sue Ann Nivens in *Mary Tyler Moore Show*, in 1975 and 1976

Emmy Award for Best Actress in a Comedy for her role as Rose Nylund in *The Golden Girls* in 1986

Seventh and last Emmy in 2010, for her performance as a guest host of *Saturday Night Live*, aged 88

Screen Actors Guild Life Achievement Award in 2010

BRIGITTE BARDOT

BORN IN PARIS, FRANCE IN 1934

In the 1950s and 1960s, she was one of the most photographed women in the world, a shining star of the French New Wave cinema and a global style icon.

'Sex symbol of France' and 'Sex kitten' were amongst her many labels. For a little context, up until 1949, wearing bikinis in the majority of Europe was banned. So, in 1952, when Brigitte Bardot had her first success in the film *Manina, the Girl in the Bikini*, she caused quite the outrage, posing in her bikini at the Cannes Festival. This ex-ballet dancer and model was comfortable in her skin and liberated fashion for women of that time.

Her film career lasted twenty years, starring in forty-eight films. Her acting career initially took off with the film *And God Created Woman* in 1956, playing the archetype of the 'femme fatale'.

BB'S BIRTH NAME WAS CAMILLE JAVEL

She refused the role of the James Bond girl:

"I think James Bond films are excellent, but without me. Unless they let me play Bond."

Film director Roger Vadim, who was her first husband, said she was "as beautiful as death, as seductive as sin and as cold as virtue."

'Independent', 'provocative', 'unconventional' are other common labels attributed to Brigitte Bardot. She was the female counterpoint to James Dean or Marlon Brando, wearing denim jeans, ballet flats and showing her neckline.

IN 1970, SHE WAS USED AS THE MODEL FOR A BUST OF MARIANNE, THE POLITICAL SYMBOL OF FRANCE AND THE FRENCH REVOLUTION. FOUR YEARS LATER ANDY WARHOL CAPTURED HER IN AN ICONIC POP ART PORTRAIT.

After retiring at forty, she created the Brigitte Bardot Foundation whose purpose is to defend animal rights and create shelters. She has been a strong animal advocate ever since. She turned ninety in 2024.

HER LEGACY IN FASHION IS SECOND TO NONE:

She asked the ballet shoe designer Repetto to create everyday ballet flats.

She popularised gingham print with her pink and white wedding dress in 1959

She spread French Riviera 'boho chic' beachwear style throughout her career, with sailor-striped shirt, capri trousers and bikinis

Her style is also associated with off-the-shoulder tops, the 'Bardot collar' to be exact.

Wild blonde hair & smoky cat eyes became her signature look

The *Brigitte Bardot Clothing Collection* launched in 2023 after she sold the rights to her name

BRONTË SISTERS:
CHARLOTTE, EMILY AND ANNE

CHARLOTTE WAS BORN IN 1816, EMILY IN 1818,
AND ANNE IN 1820, IN YORKSHIRE, UK.
EMILY DIED IN 1848; ANNE IN 1849;
AND CHARLOTTE IN 1855, ALSO IN YORKSHIRE.

The renowned Brontë sisters shared not only a passion for writing but also a fondness for cats. Felines appear throughout their works, such as Agnes Grey and Wuthering Heights, and are also mentioned in the personal diaries of Anne and Charlotte. Emily even wrote an essay in French entitled "Le Chat".

The Brontë sisters received an unusual upbringing. After their mother and their older sisters' premature deaths from illness, their father educated them at home and treated them as intellectual equals to their brother Branwell. It gave them enormous liberty to develop their imagination and roam in the Yorkshire moors together. Their novels, published under male pen names, became bestsellers during the Victorian era.

Although *Jane Eyre* is a more commonly known novel, Emily is often hailed as the literary genius of the three sisters. Her essay entitled "Le Chat", written in French whilst she was in Brussels, is of utter brilliance. Here is an English translation:

"I can say with sincerity that I like cats; I can give very good reasons why those who despise them are wrong. A cat is an animal who has more human feelings than almost any other being. We cannot sustain a comparison with the dog, it is infinitely too good; but the cat, although it differs in some physical points, is extremely like us in disposition. A cat, in its own interest, sometimes hides its misanthropy under the guise of amiable gentleness; instead of tearing what it desires from its master's hand it approaches with a caressing air [...]; and that artfulness in it is called hypocrisy. In ourselves, we give it another name, politeness, and he who did not use it to hide his real feelings would soon be driven from society. 'But,' says some delicate lady, who has murdered half a dozen lapdogs through pure affection, 'the cat is such a cruel beast, he is not content to kill his prey, he torments it before its death; you cannot make that accusation against us.' More or less, Madam. [...] You yourself avoid the bloody spectacle because it wounds your weak nerves. But I have seen you embrace your child, when he came to show you a beautiful butterfly crushed between his cruel fingers; and at that moment, I really wanted to have a cat, with the tail of a half-devoured rat hanging from its mouth to present as the image, the true copying of your angel."

EMILY BRONTË'S CAT NAMED TIGER SLEPT BY HER FEET
AS SHE WROTE *WUTHERING HEIGHTS*.

*The full essay in English can be read on page 110

CARLY RAE JEPSEN

BORN IN MISSION, CANADA IN 1985

Carly Rae Jepsen came third on Canadian Idol in 2007. She had her break with her debut album Tug of War with her instant hit "Call Me Maybe" in 2012. She has been an established pop sensation for over a decade now and a self-proclaimed Cat Lady.

First with her pastiche remake of the *Breakfast at Tiffany's* 'Cat' closing scene in her music video for "Now That I Found You" in 2019. The video features a crazy cat lady obsession with an Orangey like cat multiplying itself at every stage of her daily home life. A total revamp of the cat lady life and look: sexy, cute, young and irreverent. A modern-day fairy like vibe! She even gets a psychedelic high on a catnip + milk vape.

IN A NUTSHELL, SHE CAUGHT THE SPIRIT OF THE MILLENNIAL CAT LADY LOVE AND EMBODIED ITS NEW TAKE ON FREEDOM.

Lockdown followed and Carly Rae told a journalist of the *Guardian*, in a 2022 article published for the release of her album *The Loneliest Time*:
"Lockdown was just me, my cat, and a lot of questions about my life decisions."

This introspective life with a cat gave way to the most eclectic and personal of her albums. Yet this didn't prevent her from finding love later, and a new album called *The Loveliest Time* was released in 2023.

During her *Loneliest Time* Tour, she would post hilarious videos called "Me FaceTiming my cat every day from tour".

In addition to being a symbol of her generation, Carly Rae has become an icon in the LGBTQ+ community, with her songs "Call Me Maybe" and "Cut to the Feeling" featuring in lip sync battles in RuPaul's Drag Race and "Now That I Found You" teased in a *Queer Eye* promotional video.

Just like any dual cat nature, The A-side *Loneliest Time* found its B-side *Loveliest Time*, pandemic Mal-être turning into burning joy and desire.

A fan started a viral petition on Tumblr years ago 'Give Carly Rae Jepsen a sword,' implying that she is a slaying Queen of Pop. Ever since, she has been handed swords by fans, wooden and plastic ones, enough to make a 'Game of Thrones' chair, she once said.

CANADIAN SINGER-SONGWRITER

OVER 2.5 M FOLLOWERS ON INSTAGRAM

#CHILDLESSCATLADY

CATHERINE THE GREAT

**BORN IN STETTIN, PRUSSIA [NOW POLAND] IN 1729;
DIED NEAR ST. PETERSBURG, RUSSIA IN 1796**

Catherine II, the Empress of Russia, known as 'Catherine the Great,' reigned from 1762 to 1796. She was born Princess Sophie, daughter of Prince Christian of Analt-Zerbst, a small principality in Prussia, and raised as the future wife to Emperor Peter III, grandson of Peter the Great, Tsar of Russia. They married when she was fifteen. Peter III proved to be incompetent at ruling, siding with Prussia (he was Prussian like Catherine the Great) and stripping the clergy from their land under the guise of secularization. Catherine claimed in her memoirs that "all his actions bordered on insanity." With the help of her lover Grigory Orlov, his brothers and the support of the military class and the Russian Orthodox Church, Catherine operated a military coup in 1762, which forced Peter III to abdicate. He was assassinated a few days later.

Catherine the Great founded Russia's first state funded school for women in 1764

SHE BECAME AN EXTRAORDINARY RULER, WHO REIGNED OVER RUSSIA FOR 34 YEARS.

Greatly admired at first for her 'enlightened' ideas towards social reform, she grew more conservative and hegemonic from 1774, after hundreds of thousands of serfs and discontent peoples rebelled. Catherine the Great then consolidated powers of the nobility and expanded Russian military wars with the Ottoman Empire. Russia annexed Crimea in 1783, a strategic access point to the Black Sea.

Many rumours spread about Catherine the Great's sexual appetite. She had 12 lovers in her life, which probably for a male emperor of her time wouldn't have been noticed at all! First and foremost, she was a lady of power.

She had a special fondness for cats, with two cat colonies in the Hermitage Palace in St. Petersburg. Her personal ones were elegant Russian Blues, giving them as gifts to other sovereigns and ambassadors. Unpedigreed cats populated the basement to keep rodents away. They had official guard status, with a salary and food ration!

Prince Potemkin (military commander, statesman, and the empress's legendary lover) offered her an Angora cat to thank her for the Sèvres Cameo Service she had given him as a present, which cost the equivalent of $40 million today. She adored the cat, calling it "the cat of all cats" and "he of the velvety paws."

Her cat legacy in the Hermitage Museum is still vibrant with 70 former stray cats being housed there, roaming free in the basement and the Museum's offices, with full-time volunteers looking after them.

"Our director is always saying they are the spirit of the place," said Halttunen (a member of staff at the Hermitage Museum). "The museum's genius loci."

CLARA BARTON

BORN IN MASSACHUSETTS, USA IN 1821;
DIED IN MARYLAND, USA IN 1912

Clarissa Harlowe Barton is one of the most respected (cat) ladies in American history. She was the visionary nurse who founded the American Red Cross in 1881.

Clara Barton led an exemplary life of service, changing the lives of soldiers and their families during the Civil War. During that period, she courageously tended to soldiers, offering both medical care and much-needed supplies. Although Clara worked tirelessly from Washington, she believed she could make a greater impact closer to the front lines. In August 1862, following the Battle of Cedar Mountain in Virginia, she personally drove a four-mule team wagon from Washington to Union field hospitals to deliver essential supplies. The surgeon on duty, astonished to see a woman so near the fighting and overwhelmed by the flood of wounded soldiers, later remarked, "*I thought that night if heaven ever sent out a[n] ... angel, she must be one — her assistance was so timely.*" From that moment on, Clara became known as "The Angel of the Battlefield."

Clara's audacious and brave spirit were already at play before her exploits in the Civil War. When she was only 24 years old, she established the first free school in New Jersey in 1852. She resigned upon learning that the school had hired a man at twice her salary, declaring that she would never accept earning less than a man for the same work. She was also a passionate advocate for women's suffrage.

After the Civil War, she was given permission by President Lincoln to open 'The Office of Missing Soldiers'. From 1865 to 1868, Clara and her staff answered 63,000 letters, and provided closure for the families of 22,000 missing soldiers.

Inspired by her travels in Europe, where she had discovered the International Red Cross, she created the American Red Cross on her return in 1881. Clara dedicated herself fully to the organisation, raising funds and personally joining relief efforts — even during the Spanish-American War in Cuba at the age of 77. She led the Red Cross as its president for 23 years before retiring in 1904.

A painting of Tommy, her favourite cat, a black and white Maltese who kept her company for 17 years, hangs in the dining room of her home in Maryland, now the Clara Barton National Historic Site.

"You must never think of anything except the need, and how to meet it."

Clara Barton

Clara Barton was also well known for her love of animals, cats especially. After the Civil War, Senator Schuyler Colfax thanked her for her selfless services, with the gift of a kitten.

#CHILDLESSCATLADY

Time spent with cats is never wasted

COLETTE

BORN IN SAINT-SAUVEUR-EN-PUISAYE, FRANCE IN 1873; DIED IN PARIS, FRANCE IN 1954

"Colette - Cat owner: French novelist (1873-1954)
with a lifelong passion for cats who wrote
a number of books about her pets."

Catworld: A Feline Encyclopedia by Desmond Morris

Could Colette be the original Cat Woman?
She certainly embodies the free spirit:

"Faites des bêtises, mais faites-les avec enthousiasme"

("Do foolish things, but do them with enthusiasm")

And the sensuous symbolism: Colette had a scandalous life with many lovers...

She was often compared to a cat, with her fine traits and mysterious gaze, and was even nicknamed 'The most emancipated woman in the world'. In 1907, she caused an outrage when she performed on stage for the Moulin Rouge half naked and kissing a woman dressed as a man no other than Missy, Napoleon the III's niece and her partner at the time. She was married three times and divorced twice.

Colette was a cat lover all her life and dedicated much of her work to them. She was fascinated by their mysterious and sensual nature. In 1912, she even starred in the Music Hall *La Chatte Amoureuse* ('*The Pussy Who Was in Love*') where she was fully dressed as a cat.

In 1921, Colette wrote *Dialogues de Bêtes (Barks and Purrs)*, a collection of quirky one-act plays with two characters: a cat, Kiki-La-Doucette, and a dog, Toby-Chien.

Her short novel *La Chatte* was published in 1933. It is the story of a love triangle between a man, a woman and a cat. The cat character was inspired by Colette's favourite cat, who was a Chartreux cat. The double entendre of the 'pussy' character wasn't left unnoticed by literary critics!

In *Secrets Of The Flesh: A Life Of Colette*, by Judith Thurman, the author describes Colette's prose in this story as "particularly feline - both detached and voluptuous."

"The frizzle-headed Cat Woman of
20th-century French writing."

London Review of Books

THE CHARTREUX

One of the oldest and most cherished French cat breeds

Also favoured by the poet Charles Baudelaire and the former president Charles de Gaulle

Incredibly soft blue-grey fur

Stocky in size

Known for their silent presence - creating an exceptional complicity with their owner

IMPORTANT FACTS ABOUT COLETTE

Sidonie-Gabrielle Colette wrote more than sixty books

She was the first President of the Goncourt Academy (the most prestigious literary organisation in France)

A star of the Music Hall genre

Keira Knightley played Colette in the eponymous biopic released in 2018

DEMI MOORE

BORN IN NEW MEXICO, USA IN 1962

Demi Moore's speech for winning the Best Actress Award for
***The Substance* at the 82nd Annual Golden Globes (2025):**

"I've been doing this for a long time, over 45 years.
This is the first time I've ever won anything as an Actor"

She concluded:

"Today I celebrate this as a marker of my wholeness and
of the love that is driving me and for the gift of doing
something I love and being reminded that I do belong."

In this role, Demi Moore plays a TV host past her prime, who will take a substance that will give birth to a younger version of herself. Both bodies (the old and the young) cannot live at the same time, which will lead to a battle for survival in a dystopian, body-image obsessed, Hollywoodesque setting.

Demi, who was wildly praised and undermined at the same time for her nude scenes in the blockbusters she originally starred in, accepted playing nude scenes again, although she was 59 at the time of the shoot. It was even more impressive as she was exposed to the direct 'mirror' of the 29-year-old naked body of Margaret Qualley. Both actresses went ahead with the authenticity of their naked bodies to amplify the vulnerability of their characters on screen. This gave way to an extraordinary performance from Demi Moore.

This comeback by the actress hit the mark in an industry that has been highly criticised for its ageism towards women. Although iconic in the eighties and nineties, and having been the highest-paid actress in film history in 1996 surpassing the 10-million-dollar salary mark with the film *Striptease*, Demi Moore wasn't offered as many roles after her late thirties.

Demi was abandoned by her father before she was born. As she rose to Hollywood fame, she became well known for her daring publicity stunts, posing nude for *Vanity Fair* whilst pregnant in 1991 and again in 1992 with black body paint that resembled a man's suit.

She is praised however for defying the ageing process thanks to her fitness levels and mindfulness practice. She adores her Sphynx cats, although we have seen more of her chihuahua Pilaf on the red carpet lately. She often posts on social media with her hairless felines.

The film *The Substance* won the prize for Best Screenplay at the Cannes Film Festival in 2024. Ironically, the advertisement in the film for the product 'The Substance' is the following:

"Have you ever dreamt of a better version of yourself?"

DITA VON TEESE

Crowned the "Burlesque Superheroine" by *Vanity Fair*, **she has been featured twice in their International Best Dressed List.** She is a regular of the fashion runway, a guest star for Louis Vuitton, Chopard, Cartier, and most notably Jean-Paul Gaultier, particularly at the Fashion Freak Show in 2019 and his watershed finale in 2020.

Heather Renée Sweet took on the artist name of 'Dita Von Teese' in 1992, when she started performing. She revolutionised the art of striptease, bringing it to prime-time entertainment value, with high glamour and elegance.

The "Glamonatrix" tour showcased her iconic performances, including her signature Martini Glass routine. The show was celebrated for its stunning visuals, haute couture costumes, and custom-designed accessories.

Her eponymous lingerie collection renewed the category significantly, with its inclusive sizing and vintage silhouettes.

GRANDEST TOURS OF BURLESQUE HISTORY

"Strip, Strip, Hooray!" (2013-2016)

"The Art of the Teese" (2017)

"Dita Von Teese and the Copper Coupe" (2018)

"Glamonatrix" (2019 and 2022-2023)

Current residency at The Venetian in Las Vegas

"Diamonds & Dust: A Tale of the Good, the Bad & the Lucky" (June 2025) The Emerald Theatre in London's West End

In Paris, Dita's cat Aleister's nickname became 'chouette-souris' ('owl-mouse') because he has owl eyes and bat in French is 'chauve-souris.'

He travels with Dita on tour, as she states: "He's even been backstage with me when I am doing burlesque shows."

CAT SORORITY

Dita starred in Taylor Swift's music video for "Bejeweled." They both shimmered in diamond plated costumes and performed Dita's Martini Glass routine together with style. *Surely, they moved into the castle with their cats afterwards.*

"When I got him, his ears were huge and he didn't have much hair, just grey leathery skin, like bat-wings. He was very batty."

MEET ALEISTER, DITA'S DAPPER CAT

"Dita Von Teese's Devonshire Rex cat and art mews" (tagline on Instagram)

More than 100,000 fans on Instagram

Suave

Seductive

Stylish

"exceptionally social and brave" says Dita

Very affectionate

Plays fetch

Nickname: The Bat

Also known as "sink sitter."

Astute hunter: "One time he stole and dragged a whole chicken across the kitchen floor all the way to the living room."

Star of many photoshoots for magazines

#CHILDLESSCATLADY

DOLLY PARTON

BORN IN EAST TENNESSEE, USA IN 1946

Dolly Parton is widely recognised as a trailblazer, particularly in the country music industry, but also for her philanthropic initiatives and business acumen. She paved the way for many female country music artists after her. She successfully transitioned into pop and rock and is not slowing down. In 2023, she released her 49th album *Rockstar* and a book titled *Behind the Seams: My Life in Rhinestones,* which describes her looks and inspirations over the years.

SUPER DOLLY

Career: 60 years and counting

3,000 songs

100 million albums sold

Role model for Taylor Swift

Miley Cyrus' beloved Godmother

"It's hard to be a diamond in a rhinestone world"

She was assertive with her looks and personality from the start and made her authenticity the prime condition for the expression of her talent.

Her famous interview with the high profile journalist Barbara Walters in 1982 on ABC News, was a master class in self-esteem: "I am sure of myself as a person and I'm sure of my talent...I like the kind of person that I am so I can afford to fiddle around, diddle around with clothes and make-up and stuff, because I'm secure with myself."

Dolly believed in herself and in her talent from the start. She created her publishing company to own the publishing rights of her songs, which immensely benefited her business considering her huge hits such as "I Will Always Love You".

Dolly Parton's Imagination Library was founded in 1995 and has given access to 270 million books to children so far. Every child who is a member of the programme receives a book for free each month from birth to age 5. The charity sends two million books every month to children across sixty-seven countries. Dolly's father was illiterate, and literacy is an extremely important legacy for her. Dolly's first hit was "Dumb Blonde"... She always said she had more guts than talent!

In 2020, during the 'Black Lives Matter' riots, Dolly wrote online:

"OUR LITTLE WHITE ASSES' AREN'T ALL THAT MATTERS"

She grew an admiration as a child for a lady in her hometown who was a prostitute, and Dolly's extravagant looks have been inspired by her.

In 1971, her song "Coat of Many Colors" was taken on as a flagship anthem by the queer community.

Dolly did an iconic photo shoot with a kitten in the 1970s. Although she is not known to own a cat, she has been supporting animal rights and rescue shelters all her life. When explaining the story behind her hit song "Jolene", she said she fought the woman "like a wild cat". I think we can agree that Dolly is probably the best wild cat we know.

#CHILDLESSCATLADY

DORA MAAR

BORN IN PARIS, FRANCE IN 1907;
DIED IN PARIS, FRANCE IN 1997

When Dora Maar died, the New York Times called her "a muse of Picasso" and the "principal model for many of his so-called weeping women portraits in the late 30s and early 40s," forgetting to mention that she was an artist in her own right.

Henriette Theodora Markovitch came from a multicultural family, born from a French mother and a Croatian father. He was an ambitious architect, who decided to relocate his family to Buenos Aires, Argentina, when Theodora was only three years old. Dora grew up between Europe and Argentina. At the age of nineteen, she came to study Art in Paris at the Union Centrale des Arts Décoratifs, the École de Photographie, the Académie Julian, and the atelier of André Lhote.

In 1931, she opened a photographic studio with set designer Pierre Kéfer. Specialising in portraits, nudes, fashion and advertising, the studio was hugely successful. She was sought after by fashion luminaries such as Coco Chanel and Jeanne Lanvin, for her distinctive style using photomontages and collages. She also developed series in street photography and was friends with the likes of Henri Cartier-Bresson and Brassaï.

She became friends with André Breton's second wife Jacqueline Lamba, and became one of the few women artists included in the Surrealists' exhibitions. She was extremely talented and ambitious. She once told [the gallerist] Marcel Fleiss, "I am as good as Man Ray!"

Picasso famously painted a portrait of Dora Marr with her cat on her shoulder *Dora Maar au Chat*. The painting is the sixth highest-selling Picasso piece of all time.

As for Dora Maar, she did her own cat-inspired work, *Boy with a Cat*, a striking photograph taken as part of her series on the working class of Paris and London.

Unfortunately, her ten-year liaison with Picasso led her to stop most of her art. Instead, she was instrumental to Picasso's work, photographing every step of the creation of his monumental *Guernica* painting. She is believed to have painted the hairs (small straight lines) on the horse figure dominating the dramatic scene at the centre. This relationship slowly destroyed Dora Maar ('the weeping woman') and led her to a psychiatric hospital when it was broken off. Thanks to the help of her friend the poet Paul Éluard, she was transferred to the clinic of psychoanalyst Jacques Lacan.

SHE WAS STILL PAINTING IN HER EIGHTIES AND FINALLY GAINED RECOGNITION IN RECENT YEARS.

In 2019, after it was first held in Pompidou in Paris, a major retrospective was held at London's Tate Modern, featuring nearly 300 objects: photographs, photomontages, advertising mock-ups, self-portraits, watercolours, oil landscapes and still lifes.

'us females
are a feline
breed'

EARTHA KITT

**BORN IN SOUTH CAROLINA, USA IN 1927;
DIED IN CONNECTICUT, USA IN 2008**

*"Believe me, baby, this pussy cat knows how to scratch
and bite," Eartha told a journalist in 1987. "After all,
I've had to claw my way up from the very start."*

As we can see in this book, Eartha Kitt is not the first cat lady with a difficult childhood. An out-of-wedlock child of a Cherokee and African American mother, she never knew her white father. However, she wasn't raised by her mother as she died when Eartha was still a young child. She grew up for the first part of her youth in a foster home, where she was neglected and abused. Thankfully, her aunt took her in for the second part of her childhood in New York City. A world of opportunities opened to her when she joined, at sixteen, Katherine Dunham's pioneering African American dance troop which was touring in North America and Europe. She decided to start her solo career. She was so talented Orson Welles called her "the most exciting girl in the world." She was known as a 'sultry' singer and an exceptional performer. With early 1950s recordings such as "C'est Si Bon," "Santa Baby," and "I Want to Be Evil," Kitt became a star.

She also became the first Black woman on prime-time TV in the 1960s, with her role as Catwoman in the hit series *Batman*.

Her sexy skintight catsuit and signature "purr" consolidated her reputation as 'sex kitten.'

KITT LOVED CATS OFF SCREEN TOO AND WOULD TAKE HER BLACK CAT JINX EVERYWHERE, INCLUDING BACKSTAGE AT LIVE PERFORMANCES.

She was a Civil Rights activist and joined the group Rebels with a Cause.

Her showbiz career took a hit after she confronted President Johnson and the first lady at a luncheon in the White House, about teenage crime and the Vietnam War in 1968.

In 1975, the *New York Times* asked for her permission to publish a 1950s CIA report that was written about her, where she was condemned for her "loose morals," and described as a "sadistic nymphomaniac," which were all biased assumptions based on the colour of her skin and her then single status.

The title of her last memoir is *I'm Still Here: Confessions of a Sex Kitten* (1989), and she is now recognised by millennials as the voice of villain Yzma in Disney's 2000 cartoon *The Emperor's New Groove*, for which she won an Emmy.

"They don't understand that I don't think of myself in terms of being a black person {...}. I think of myself as being a person who belongs to everybody, but I think one should always feel this way."

"I HAVE USED ALL THE MANURE THAT HAS BEEN THROWN ON ME AS *FERTILIZER* TO MAKE ME STRONGER."

ELINOR GLYN

**BORN IN JERSEY, CHANNEL ISLANDS IN 1864;
DIED IN LONDON, UK IN 1943**

Cats are known as best companions to women who write or read.

The famous saying remains:

*"A woman cannot survive on books alone.
She also needs a cat."*

Elinor Glyn was the British queen of romantic fiction in the early twentieth century. She was a pioneer in the hugely popular genre known today as 'new romance' or 'new adult'.

Her *risqué* and scandalous novel *Three Weeks*, published in 1907, sold more than two million copies.

Following the success of her novels, she was signed as a scriptwriter in Hollywood in 1920, where she initiated the concept of the 'It-girl'. The film *It* was the adaptation of her eponymous hit novel, which propelled Clara Bow to super stardom.

IT BECAME SYNONYMOUS WITH SEX APPEAL. EITHER YOU HAVE *IT* OR YOU DON'T.

This is how Elinor Glyn defined 'It' during an interview on British Movietone News:

"Have you ever seen a tiger in a zoo? [...] Watch how it lies there, utterly indifferent, doesn't care an atom who's passing, who's going to give him a biscuit or get away in fear. It just stays there gazing, looking straight into the eyes of whoever is looking at it."

She wanted to make the point that it was the opposite of being self-conscious.

She also described it as follows:

"In the animal world 'It' demonstrates in tigers and cats — both animals being fascinating and mysterious, and quite unbiddable."

Elinor had two mysterious and fascinating cats of her own, Candid and Zadig. They were marmalade-coloured cats, like mirrors to Elinor's red hair and fiery temper.

In *Three Weeks*, the book's most famous scene was a sex scene that took place on a tiger skin:

"Beautiful one! beautiful one!' she purred. 'And I know all your feelings and your passions, and now I have got your skin—for the joy of my skin!' And she quivered again with the movements of a snake."

This led to a popular anonymous verse:

*Would you like to sin
With Elinor Glyn
On a tiger skin?
Or would you prefer
To err with her
On some other fur?*

Women's sexual freedom was taboo and unspoken of in those times. Elinor Glyn was a literary trailblazer in that respect.

Also celebrated for her good looks even in her late sixties, her famous beauty tip was to scrub your face with a dry nail brush until it appeared crimson!

"HER OBITUARY READ THAT SHE WAS 'A ROMANTIC...AND SHE LIVED AN INTENSE AND ADVENTUROUS LIFE."

One of the most iconic photographs of Princess Elizabeth Bibesco was taken with a black cat in 1930.

PRINCESS ELIZABETH BIBESCO

BORN IN LONDON, UK IN 1897;
DIED IN BUCHAREST, ROMANIA IN 1945

DAUGHTER OF SIR HERBERT HENRY ASQUITH, PRIME MINISTER OF GREAT BRITAIN BETWEEN 1908 AND 1916, AND WIFE OF PRINCE ANTOINE BIBESCO FROM ROMANIA.

Princess Elizabeth Bibesco was a novelist from the 1920s, contemporary to Virginia Woolf, symbolic of a 'lost era' and a decadent Central European aristocracy.

Although forgotten in literary history, she held a firm place in literary circles at the time and in the rise of Impressionist and Modernist literature. Virginia Woolf's Bloomsbury Circle despised her for being a socialite rather than a writer, but Elizabeth Bibesco was close to Marcel Proust, who was an intimate friend of her husband Prince Antoine Bibesco, and was very much influenced by the Impressionist literary principles. Like Proust, "Antoine Bibesco had chosen to turn his life into a work of art" (wrote Palewski in 1974), and so did his wife.

Proust wrote to Antoine Bibesco: "I think that it is only to the involuntary memories that the artist should demand the raw material of his work".

Marcel Proust wrote in *Pastiches et mélanges*:

"Miss Asquith who was probably the most intelligent of all and looked like one of those beautiful figures from the frescoes one can see in Italy, got married to Prince Antoine Bibesco who had been the idol of those where he had lived. The wedding was very popular and there were cheers from everywhere" (1919)

Unfortunately, the famously handsome Prince Antoine Bibesco was unfaithful and led Elizabeth to a tragic marriage. She sought comfort in alcohol and lovers' arms. When World War II broke out, Elizabeth and her husband were in Romania, where she is said to have died in April 1945, while listening to war news on the BBC.

Maurice Schumann summed up her tragic life in these words:

"Extravagant, generous and liberal, Elizabeth seemed to foresee the cruelty of her destiny: she was to die in a Romania forced to join the camp of her country's enemies and she was never to see again the flowers from Kew Gardens or the apses of Notre Dame."

Nevertheless, she tirelessly worked for the wounded heroes of the war, for whom she organised many charity matinees.

Her 'black cat' like spirit is very well captured in her epitaph, the last line of her last poem in her 1927 collection reading:

"My soul has gained the freedom of the night"

ELIZABETH TAYLOR

BORN IN LONDON, UK IN 1932;
DIED IN LOS ANGELES, USA IN 2011

ELIZABETH TAYLOR WAS THE RECIPIENT OF
A STRING OF LABELS THROUGHOUT HER
LIFE AS A MOVIE STAR:

'THE LEGEND'
'THE PHENOMENON'
'SEX SYMBOL'
'QUEEN ELIZABETH'

In *Elizabeth Taylor, the Lost Tapes*, Elizabeth said "One is flesh and blood, and one is cellophane."

She is said to be the last major star of the old Hollywood studio era. Although she was born in England, her American parents moved the family back to the United States at the start of the Second World War in 1939, where they settled in Los Angeles. Already strikingly beautiful, Elizabeth Taylor started acting at the age of ten. She then became MGM's top child star with the smash hit "National Velvet" in 1944.

> "I fought against the studios and started
> to make my own deals. I was quite
> a business woman!"
>
> *Elizabeth Taylor, the Lost Tapes*

Elizabeth Taylor was an exceptional actress and won two Oscars, one for her performance in *Butterfield 8* (1960) and one for her role in *Who's Afraid of Virginia Woolf?* (1966). She is mostly remembered for her title role in *Cleopatra* (1963), which was one of the most expensive productions of all time.

Elizabeth Taylor was a cat lover all her life. On a safari in Africa, she came across a rare black-maned lion. The safari guide told her not to lock eyes because lions consider that as a threat, but she couldn't take her eyes off the lion. After a few minutes, the lion stretched and walked away, glancing back at Liz over his shoulder along the way. Liz Taylor's magnetic 'velvet' eyes seemed to be the exception to the lion's rule...

Elizabeth Taylor and James Dean became good friends on the set of *Giant* (1955), and she gave him a Siamese cat he named Marcus.

For two months in 1974, Elizabeth Taylor and Richard Burton, her husband at the time, moved to California with Cassius, just one of Liz's many beloved cats. It unfortunately went missing and Liz wrote:

"*Letter to my Lovely
Lost Cat*

*I see you, my beauty boy,
in the reflection of those
shining black-brown
rocks ahead of me. I see
the green o' thy eyes in
every rained, sweated leaf
shaking in my eyes.*

*I remember the sweet
smell of your fur against
my neck when I was
deeply in trouble and how,
somehow you made it
better — you knew!
You knew always when
I hurt and you made
comfort for me, as I did
once for you when you
were a broken kitten.*

*Anyway, I love you
Cassius — and thank you
for your beauty.*

Please come back!"

Ellen DeGeneres started her career as a stand-up comedian and was voted 'Funniest Person in America' in 1982. In 1994, Ellen headlined a sitcom on ABC called *These Friends of Mine* (renamed *Ellen* after its first season). She made TV history in 1997, when her character, and Ellen personally, came out as a lesbian. Some of the sponsors suspended their advertisements and Ellen became persona non grata in Hollywood for a couple of years. Thankfully, she was able to host a new talk show launched in 2003 called *Ellen: The Ellen DeGeneres Show*, which quickly became a huge success. It received 15 Emmy Awards during its first three seasons on air.

"I'm a lesbian, an Aquarius, and a vegetarian."

Ellen DeGeneres

Ellen was awarded the Presidential Medal of Freedom by Barack Obama in 2016. The President said these precious words about Ellen:

"Ellen DeGeneres has a way of making you laugh about something, rather than at someone [...] think of the courage it took for Ellen to come out on the most public of stages, almost 20 years ago, just how important it was, not just to the LGBT community but to all of us [...] to risk your career like that, people don't do that very often"

She would always end her show with "Be kind to one another". Sadly, her 19-year show was ended in May 2022 due to allegations of a toxic workplace. This was devastating for Ellen, who publicly took responsibility, although she hadn't been aware of it and was deeply affected. Again, she was made persona non grata. When someone in the audience of her last show asked if she would seek revenge, she replied again with a spirit of kindness: "I really don't hold on to stuff. It's just not who I am."

During her daily show, Ellen was a recurrent animal advocate, and cats had a very special place in her show. For many years, she celebrated 'Cat Week' with 'Best Cat Videos' and other jokes/sketches centred around cats. She even called an online cat sensation for its birthday (after the owner issued a comedic video of the cat asking for it). As her cat had been declared 'too fat' by her vet, Ellen made a tribute to 'fat cats', with best videos of these big bosses. Her hilarious sketch "Kitty corner" with Taylor Swift, featuring both of them as the ultimate cat ladies, remains a classic of the show.

ELLEN HAS HAD SEVERAL CATS. SHE ADORED ONE IN PARTICULAR NAMED CHARLIE, AND SHE EXPRESSED HER DEEP GRIEF ON SOCIAL MEDIA WHEN HE PASSED. SINCE 2023, SHE HAS TWO NEW RESCUE CATS, JINK AND MONKEY.

#CHILDLESSCATLADY

ENYA

BORN IN COUNTY DONEGAL, IRELAND IN 1961

Enya started out in her siblings' Celtic music band Clannad. She broke away to become a solo artist, sponsored by Clannad's previous producer, Nicky Ryan and his wife Roma. They have been working together ever since.

Enya is known to be a very private musician, living in her 19th century castle in Killiney, south of Dublin. After several traumatic events involving deranged fans, she has made less and less public appearances. To the 'recluse' label often attributed to her, she replies:

"I am not reclusive. I just have a private life.'
'I don't need a man in my life."

She is known to spend most of her days in her studio, creating her unique ethereal sound, a mix of layered recordings of her own voice, with influences from classical, Celtic and ambient music. Her songs are in English, Gaelic but also in Sindarin and Quenya, languages that J.R.R. Tolkien created for *The Lord of the Rings*, and Loxian, which she invented herself with her songwriters. Along with a few staff and cats (she had twelve at once at one point) and rare visitors to her castle, her life is centred around music creation:

"I'm too much devoted to my music.
Some people think it sounds sad but
believe me, I'm happy. I am my music."

In March 2025, Enya issued the following statement about the award she received at the RTE Choice Music Prize for her 1988 *Watermark* album:

"I am very very honoured tonight," she said. "When Watermark came out, I was just so proud to be able to make music. My love of music has always been a driving force to me and any success always feels like a great bonus, as I've been determined to create music which is true to myself from a very young age. Watermark really kickstarted my career and has always remained very special to me."

IMPORTANT FACTS ABOUT ENYA

Born Eithne Pádraigin Ni Bhraonáin; the English pronunciation of her Gaelic name Eithne is Enya

Has sold more than 80 million albums worldwide

Estimated fortune at 140 million euros. She is believed to be the richest woman in British and Irish music history

Her break in the United States came with her song "Only Time," which was aired by CNN as the background music to the footage of the 9/11 attacks

Ireland's bestselling solo artist

Four Grammy awards and six World Music Awards

More than 38 years after the release of her self-titled album, her music is still going viral on Tik Tok, X and other socials

Enya has co-owned a music company, Aigle Music, with Nicky and Roma Ryan since 1981

FLORENCE NIGHTINGALE

BORN IN FLORENCE, ITALY IN 1820;
DIED IN LONDON, UK IN 1910

An icon of Victorian culture, Florence Nightingale is the founder of modern nursing in the United Kingdom, as well as a famous cat lady of her time.

Victorian education taught women that marriage was the purpose of life. Florence however was educated privately with her sister by their father and learned to think independently. From a very early age, she became an avid reader. When she refused to marry at the age of 24, it was quite revolutionary for her time.

As a matter of fact, Victorian law gave single women the same rights as men. They could acquire property, assume responsibilities for their debts, enter a contract, make a will, sue and be sued.

In 1765, the English jurist William Blackstone famously wrote:

"By marriage, the very being or legal existence of a woman is suspended or at least incorporated or consolidated into that of the husband, under whose wing, protection, or cover she performs everything, and she is therefore called in our law a feme covert."

Florence became known as 'The Lady with the Lamp' during the Crimean War, where she transformed the hygiene conditions of the soldiers' hospital wards and significantly improved the survival rate. There, a soldier gave her a cat to help control rats in the hospital facilities. She also started to notice the benefits of animal therapy on soldiers. She was hailed as a hero when she returned to Britain.

In addition, Florence Nightingale was recently celebrated as 'The Cat Lady with the Lamp.' In a letter put up for auction, she declared her affection for Mr Bismarck, a Persian tom cat who is believed to have been her favourite.

She wrote: *"Should you know of a cat fancier who would like a very handsome thoroughbred, powerful Tom cat, a Persian, about a year old, Mr Bismarck by name, black brown and yellow, without a speck of white, who will follow like a dog.*

A great pet. I am looking for a very good home for my Bismarck, whom I cannot keep. He was sent down to me from London a day or two ago because the lady who asked me for him could not take him abroad. Pray excuse this question."

She eventually took Mr Bismarck in and was known to serve him specially prepared food on china plates.

During her lifetime, Florence Nightingale lived with 60 cats, including 17 at once. She let them walk freely around the house and added their ink paw prints on many of her letters. For the last two decades of her life, Nightingale was bedridden, and she would let her cats lay on her pillow. She carefully made arrangements in her will for the cats' ongoing care.

In 1856, Queen Victoria wrote to her hoping to "make the acquaintance of one who has set so bright an example to our sex."

FLORENCE NIGHTINGALE WAS THE FIRST WOMAN TO RECEIVE THE BRITISH HONOUR OF THE ORDER OF MERIT IN 1907.

GEORGIA O'KEEFFE

Very few women artists have received such status and level of recognition as Georgia O'Keeffe did in her lifetime. Even in the 21st century, she is still one of the top selling artists, with Jimson Weed/White Flower No. 1 selling at $44.4 million in 2014, setting a record for the most expensive artwork by a female artist ever sold at auction.

Georgia O'Keeffe was a pioneering artist in the first half of the 20th century. She was sure of her talent and her first solo exhibition at Alfred Stieglitz's gallery in 1917 in New York City, was immediately a success. Critics instantly applied a gender label to her paintings, where they saw an ode to the vulva. O'Keeffe deeply disagreed with such a vision and always placed her art above gender.

As an art student in New York City, Georgia O'Keeffe befriended a group of avant-garde male artists such as Arthur Garfield Dove, John Marin and Paul Strand.

Georgia stayed 'Miss O'Keeffe' all her life, although she married the gallerist and photographer Alfred Stieglitz in 1924.

Her very close friend was Anita Pollitzer, suffragette and President of the Women's Party in 1945.

Georgia remained an independent woman in spirit, singular in art, with a strong personality. A true Cat Lady!

She adored cats, particularly Siamese, and included them in her life and art. She wrote the following in a letter to Alfred Stieglitz in the summer of 1944:
"We also got the cat –she is a very beautiful cat –dainty and beautiful –quite a dark Siamese –So now we have the cat."

Georgia had several Siamese cats, and they are much featured in letters and photographs. One particular cat was named The Gato ('the cat' in Spanish) and there are photographs of her smiling and holding it in her arms in Abiquiu, in 1941.

Christine Taylor Patten, who was Georgia O'Keeffe's carer at the end of her life, said in a 2016 BBC documentary:
"She was a very kind, intelligent, generous, clear woman."

As Patten describes it, the artist possessed a kind of 'wholeness' that, having refused all distractions, dwells fully, like a cat: still, awake, and content to remain sitting with herself.

(HTTPS://MYGEORGIAOKEEFFE.COM/S BLOG)

This quote by Goethe encapsulates Georgia O'Keeffe's passion very well:
"This is the highest wisdom that I own; freedom and life are earned by those alone who conquer them each day anew."

GINA GERSHON

GINA GERSHON HAS CALLED HERSELF A 'CRAZY CAT LADY' AFTER EMBARKING ON A DESPERATE SEARCH FOR HER BLACK CAT CLEO, HAVING JUST BROKEN UP WITH HER BOYFRIEND.

Her book *In Search of Cleo: How I Found My Pussy and Lost My Mind* was published in 2012 and tells of her trials and tribulations looking for Cleo, a metaphor for her lost lovers and past relationships.

Gina Gershon is known for being a character actress, having had her break in Hollywood as queer characters in *Showgirls* (1995) and *Bound* (1996). Her agent told her that playing lesbian characters would ruin her career... at sixty-two years old, Gina remains highly solicited for a female actress of her age, playing in numerous TV and streaming platform shows like *How to Make it in America*, as well as films like *Borderlands*.

For her queer part in *Showgirls*, she said:

"I decided to make my part campy because I initially thought that it was going to be really dark and really intense and then it just turned out to be completely different. So instead of going in that direction, I decided to make it so that drag queens would want to dress as my character on Halloween."

Her novel *In Search of Cleo: How I Found My Pussy and Lost My Mind* starts with the quote:

"'All I wanted to do was take off my Euro-wear and cuddle with my best friend of three years, my kitty cat Cleo. Cleohold, keeper of my heart, truth of my soul, my bud, my beast."

When her assistant loses her beloved cat Cleo, Gina spends two months roaming the back streets of Los Angeles at all hours of the night, in search of Cleo. This will be the background to an adventure into LA's subcultures, meeting Ellen DeGeneres' animal psychic Sonia; listening to Arthur the newspaper delivery man's special advice; a mysterious fortune teller, who gives her a statue of Saint Gertrude, the protector of cats; chanting with hippies; being slapped with a chicken by a Santeria priest... the book will delight singletons and pet lovers as Gina chases her sanity and black male cat Cleo, her precious soul mate.

GINA GERSHON HAS INDEED ESTABLISHED HERSELF AS A QUEEN OF AMERICAN CAMP.

GLORIA STEINEM

BORN IN OHIO, USA IN 1934

Gloria Steinem made headlines in 1963 with her "A Bunny's Tale" report as an undercover journalist in the Playboy Bunny Club in New York City. This kicked off her career, shaking one of the highest symbols of patriarchy in America. She became the face of the Women's Rights Movement in the 1970s. Together with Brenda Feigen Fasteau and Dorothy Pitman Hughes, she established the Women's Action Alliance (WAA) in 1971. The organisations mission was to empower women and combat sexism by coordinating resources for grassroots initiatives and individuals involved in the women's movement. She was also the co-founder of Ms Magazine with Dorothy Pitman Hughes, one of the US's first women's magazines aiming at spreading feminist values and political awareness, such as democratic families and reproductive freedom.

"The truth will set you free, but first it will piss you off."

"I would say that each of us has only one thing to gain from the feminist movement: Our whole humanity."

Gloria Steinem spent most of her life traveling, meeting and discussing with women all over the world, writing essays and books rich from her experiences. She praised self-esteem and self-love, sorority and personal freedom. A far cry from clichés about women that persist today, such as women relishing in cat fights and crazy behaviours. She disagreed with the premise of the recent TV series *Mrs America*, treating the history of feminism as a cradle for female competition.

Gloria has owned several cats throughout her life. Her favourite was her Persian named Magritte, which she said taught her about "strong will and self-authority." When Gloria was asked in 2017 about how to raise the next generation of women and girls, she suggested taking our cues from cats: "Cats don't let you touch them. Cats tell you what they're going to do, and that's that."

Gloria Steinem calls cats "a writer's most logical and agreeable companion."

WRITTEN WORKS

The Truth Will Set You Free, But First It Will Piss You Off (2019)

My Life on the Road (2015)

Doing Sixty & Seventy (2014)

As If Women Matter: The Essential Gloria Steinem Reader (2014)

Marilyn (2013)

Revolution from Within (2012)

Moving Beyond Words (1994)

Outrageous Acts and Everyday Rebellions (1983)

The Beach Book (1963)

#CHILDLESSCATLADY

GRACE KELLY

BORN IN PHILADELPHIA, USA IN 1929;
DIED IN MONACO, IN 1982

'The Hollywood Dream Girl' Grace Kelly came from an affluent, athletic, Irish American family in Philadelphia.

Her father was a triple Olympic champion and her mother a swimming coach at university. Despite being raised with a silver spoon, Grace Kelly had a difficult childhood. Her mother was abusive physically and her father mostly absent and challenging. "*We were always competing for everything - competing for love,*" she once said. Luckily, she was inspired by her uncle George Kelly, an actor turned playwright who won a Pulitzer Prize in 1926. He was instrumental in getting her an audition at the American Academy of Dramatic Arts in New York, where she came to train as an actor.

Grace Kelly featured in 60 television dramas before she started her career as a Hollywood star. Alfred Hitchcock took her under his wing and she played in three of his films consecutively: *Rear Window* in 1954, alongside James Stewart; *Dial M for Murder* that same year; and *To Catch a Thief* in 1956, with Cary Grant. Interestingly the latter played the role of John Robie "The Cat", and Grace Kelly's character identifies him as "The Cat burglar" in a famous scene where she's speeding down the narrow roads of the French Riviera with him in the front passenger seat. Film buffs debate whether a subliminal shot of a black cat was cut in that scene for later versions of the movie.

IF WE LOOK AT THE REAR-VIEW MIRROR OF GRACE KELLY'S CAT LADY LIFE, IT TAKES US BACK TO 1948, WHEN SHE WAS PHOTOGRAPHED WITH HER KITTEN FOR A MAGAZINE WHEN SHE WAS A PART-TIME MODEL.

Fast forward to her life as Her Serene Highness Princess Grace of Monaco, when she owned three cats Bibby, Button, and Toulouse.

"She was a complete trailblazer — modelling, acting and brands as well," said Gemma Godfrey, who contributed to the documentary *Grace Kelly: The Missing Millions*. Sadly, Grace Kelly had to give up her film career when she married Prince Rainier of Monaco in 1956, 'the Wedding of the Century' viewed on television by 30 million people. It was one year after she had won an Oscar for her role in *Country Girl* (1955), her career was at its peak.

Nevertheless, Hollywood did not forget her. She remained 'One of the most beautiful women in the world', an icon of glamour and timeless elegance. After her tragic death in a car accident, James Stewart said in his eulogy: "*I just love Grace Kelly, not because she was a Princess, not because she was an actress, not because she was my friend, but because she was just about the nicest lady I ever met.*"

HANNAH SHAW

BORN IN THE USA, IN 1987

Hannah René Shaw – a.k.a The Kitten Lady is the true badass of today's cat world. With her tattooed body and giant smile, this millennial and kitten hero could well be one of the top champions of childless cat lady coolness.

Awarded Advocate of the Year at CatCon Worldwide in 2017 and Cat Advocate of the Year by ASPCA (American Society for the Prevention of Cruelty to Animals) in 2019, she is the go-to educator for kitten rescue and training. With more than 4 million followers on her social media accounts and YouTube channel, her videos are instrumental to cat lovers who search online resources for adopting and raising kittens. With her wealth of experience in instructional workshops and consulting services, she wrote the New York Times bestseller *Tiny but Mighty: Kitten Lady's Guide to Saving the Most Vulnerable Felines.*

Hannah Shaw is the founder of Orphan Kitten Club, a nonprofit organisation dedicated to revolutionising kitten welfare in the United States. Through shelter grants, ethical pediatric research, and direct care for vulnerable neonates, the organization is driving meaningful change. Since 2019, it has awarded over $3 million in targeted funding to help shelters create innovative and life-saving programmes for kittens.

"THERE ARE NO ORDINARY CATS."

Hannah studied psychology at university and was working in various cat rescue organisations, when she started the Orphan Kitten Club and her own kitten welfare channel online. Almost ten years later, she has been hailed as an expert on Animal Planet and has received multiple awards. To topple all this, a match made in heaven was made possible in cat world. Hannah and cat photographer Andrew Marttila got married on a farm in California in 2019. Some of the highlights were a flowered basket of new calico rescue kittens from the bride to the groom and their pig Hugo featuring as the ring bearer (he was lured by popcorn thrown by the flower girl). Their cats Coco and Eloise unfortunately couldn't attend.

ABOUT *CATCON*:
"It's like Comic-con but for Cat People"
Laughing Squid

The couple lately travelled to 30 countries around the world to capture cat culture and welfare, with snappy shots of cats who know how to pose in front of monuments or atmospheric places. This new book is called *Cats of the World* and was published in October 2024. It's already a New York Times bestseller.

According to womansworld.com, Hannah Shaw has fostered over 1,000 kittens in the past 16 years that she has specialised in this field.

#CHILDLESSCATLADY

HELEN CHANDLER

BORN IN SOUTH CAROLINA, USA IN 1906; DIED IN LOS ANGELES, USA IN 1965

'Although largely forgotten today, Helen Chandler was propelled to international fame close to 100 years ago, with the first film iteration of Dracula in 1931. She was paid more to star in that film than her co-star Bela Lugosi, who had already played the role of Count Dracula on the Broadway stage production.

Helen Chandler had returned to movies in the thirties with the popularity of the talkies. She had played in silent films before but much preferred the stage. Together with her brother, she had been brought up by her mother to become a 'star child'. She was 8 years old for her first role on stage and 12 for her first role in Broadway. She soon became a well-known Broadway actress. Unfortunately, she suffered all her life from the harsh upbringing she received from her mother. Yes, she became a professional at a young age, with high resilience and confidence (she had appendicitis throughout the 6 weeks of shooting *Dracula* and waited to get surgery until the last day on set), but she suffered from alcoholism and lived through 3 unhappy marriages. She was sadly committed to an asylum in the 1950s. Little is known about Helen Chandler's personal life, although she was a true movie legend of her time. The fragments that still appear are notably endearing pictures of her at home, with her cat Blue Bell.

She died prematurely in her late fifties (the exact year of her birth is still unclear, between 1906 and 1908) and no family members claimed her ashes. As a result, her urn was locked away in a private vault in the Chapel of the Pines in Los Angeles. Thanks to her fan club, it was recently given a niche in the Cathedral Mausoleum of Hollywood Forever Cemetery. Now classic horror film fans can access the resting place of *Mina* played by the once legendary Helen Chandler.

The beautiful chiaroscuro aesthetic of the film magnified her character's immaculate complexion and ethereal allure.

The *New York Times* review read at the time:

"Helen Chandler gives an excellent performance as one of the girls who is attacked by the 'undead Count.' [...] This picture can at least boast of being the best of the many mystery films."

"I am all in a sea of wonders. I doubt; I fear; I think strange things, which I dare not confess to my own soul"

Bram Stoker, *Dracula*

#CHILDLESSCATLADY

HELEN MIRREN

BORN IN LONDON, UK IN 1945

"A serious actress can't have big bosoms, is that what you mean?"

Helen Mirren responding to Michael Parkinson on his chat show in 1975

Born from a Russian father, whose aristocratic family had fled the Bolshevik Revolution, and a Scottish mother, Helen Mironoff became Helen Mirren at the age of ten, when her father anglicised their family name. She joined Britain's National Youth Theatre at the age of 18 and became a member of the Royal Shakespeare Company a year later.

"No matter what sex you are, be a feminist"

(Helen Mirren, commencement speech at Tulane University)

From the early years of her career Helen Mirren endured sexist remarks on a regular basis. She handled them with incredible wit, humour and grace.

Dame Helen Mirren has played in 130 films and television roles, as well as 40 stage productions.

It was only in her forties that she became an international star on screen, with her television role of detective Jane Tennison in the *Prime Suspect* series (1991–96, 2003 and 2006), an adaptation of the bestselling thrillers by Lynda La Plante. At the time, it was very rare to have a TV series led by a single woman.

Long before (in 1976), Helen Mirren had played a stage role of the passionate cat lady Stella in *The Collection*, by Harold Pinter. Her character owned a longhaired white cat, which was seen with her throughout the play.

Helen has always been a vocal supporter for animal rights, raising awareness about issues such as factory farming, the cruelty involved in fur production, but also trophy hunting and the exploitation of wild animals. In addition, she has also been an activist for human rights championing foster care and adoption, fighting against child poverty, sexual exploitation and domestic violence.

Best Actress award at the Cannes Film Festival for her role in *Northern Ireland* (1984)

Oscar for Best Actress for her role as Queen Elizabeth II, in *The Queen* (2007)

BAFTA for Best Actress for her role in *The Queen* (2007)

Four Emmy Awards for her work in *Prime Suspect* (1999) and *The Passion of Ayn Rand* (2006), and then for her role in *The Queen* (2007)

Dame Commander of the Order of the British Empire (DBE) in 2003

Tony Award for Leading Actress in *The Audience*, where she reprised her Oscar-winning portrayal of Queen Elizabeth II on Broadway (2015)

HELEN MIRREN WEARS A TATTOO ON HER HAND, WHICH READS IN MAYAN ANCIENT LANGUAGE:

"Inlakesh" ("You are my other self; I am another yourself")

Her cat's name is Tallinn.

HILARY SWANK

BORN IN NEBRASKA, USA IN 1974

Hilary Ann Swank moved to Los Angeles with her mother in 1990, where she started acting professionally. Her breakout role was in *The Next Karate Kid* in 1994. She won two Oscars as Best Actress for playing Brandon Teena in *Boys Don't Cry* (1999) and the boxing champion Maggie Fitzgerald in *Million Dollar Baby* (2004), directed by Clint Eastwood. *Million Dollar Baby* also won Oscars for Best Motion Picture, Best Performance by an Actor in a Supporting Role (Morgan Freeman) and Best Achievement in Directing (Clint Eastwood).

Million Dollar Baby tells the story of Maggie, a 31-year-old waitress in Missouri, who always dreamed of becoming a professional boxer. Ill-tempered Frankie Dunn (Clint Eastwood), a veteran Los Angeles boxing trainer keeping most people at arm's length, will eventually accept to train Maggie.

'Every day when I look at my pets, I know they're thankful I've adopted them. I'm just as thankful they've adopted me.'

"There's such an art to boxing, it's like a great game of chess. When you're in the ring, you're one with your opponent. Everything goes silent and it's you and that person. You hear your breath. You hear the other person. And as you try to figure out their strength and weakness, you're learning about your own strength and weaknesses. And each person that you spar or fight with, their strength and weakness brings out new strength and weakness in yourself. And the second you think, 'I have this person,' and get cocky, you can lose and you usually do. It's a great analogy to life. You have to remain humble and have respect for the other person."

Hilary Swank was the first woman to receive an Oscar for a role as a boxer. She is the third youngest woman in history to win two Academy Awards.

She is also known to have many animals and pets. She describes them as "her family." She volunteered many years at ASPCA (American Society for the Prevention of Cruelty to Animals). As part of their campaign for help after the 9/11 attacks, she rescued a terrified kitten from a smoke-damaged apartment nearby the fallen twin towers. She was seen in October 2009 cuddling cats, taking part in a New York Bideawee Animal Shelter event to promote pet adoption. A former ambassador for Iams cat food, she has also been a voice for the "Shelter Me: In Times of Need" programme, which partners Alzheimer's facilities with animal shelters, enabling residents to foster newborn kittens.

IN 2015, SHE STARTED THE HILAROO FOUNDATION THAT BRINGS TOGETHER ANIMALS IN NEED OF CARE AND DISADVANTAGED YOUTH. SHE HAS RECENTLY BEEN AWARDED THE COMPASSION AWARD BY ASPCA.

JANE FONDA

BORN IN NEW YORK CITY, USA IN 1937

One of the 20th century's highest profiles, Jane Fonda, had a tragic childhood, brought up by a temperamental father, the legendary actor Henry Fonda, and a mother who committed suicide when Jane was only 13 years old. She revealed it all in her autobiography *My Life So Far*, published in 2005, which sold more than a million copies in the United States in the year of its release.

Like many cats, Jane Fonda has had many lives. She learnt French with her first husband, film director Roger Vadim. She was one of the few American women to feature in French New Wave films. She was a Civil Rights activist and campaigned against the Vietnam War. She wasn't a feminist but became one in her later years. She turned into a fitness star in her forties. She not only acted in films but produced some, namely the last film starring Henry Fonda, *On Golden Pond* (1981), where she played alongside him. She became a climate activist, known for her 'Fire Drill Fridays' protests, which she started in 2019, inspired by Greta Thunberg.

French journalist Pauline Klein wrote "Jane Fonda could be the incarnation of America's contradictions."

"Being an activist and being as controversial as I am doesn't mean that you have to suddenly be ugly and boring and not care how you look"

she told a journalist at the 78th annual Cannes Film Festival.

At 87, she is an ambassador for a range of hair products by L'Oréal Paris and wears hers proud and shiny grey.

Jane Fonda has had multiple cats throughout her life, a black cat in particular named Snickers and a wild tuxedo cat named Shadow. Shadow may echo the mesmerising opening scene of one of Jane Fonda's early movies, *Walk on the Wild Side* (1962). It starts with a black and white travelling shot of a black cat casting its shadow on a pavement at night, with iconic music in the background by Elmer Bernstein. *Les Félins*, literally *The Felines*, followed in 1964 with Alain Delon, and *Cat Ballou* in 1965.

IMPORTANT FACTS ABOUT JANE FONDA'S MANY LIVES

Trained at Actors Studio alongside Marilyn Monroe, under the tutelage of Lee Strasberg

Starred in risqué French film *Barbarella* (1968)

From the 1970s, her political and social activism never stopped: fighting for First Nations, Civil Rights, protesting against the war in Vietnam, defending abortion rights, raising awareness for climate change

Won 2 Oscars: one for *Klute* (1971) and one for *Coming Home* (1978)

Jane Fonda's Workout Book sold more than 17 million copies worldwide

Lifetime Achievement Award from the Screen Actors Guild (2025)

'Empathy is not weak or woke.'

JANE FONDA AT THE SAG AWARDS, 2025

JEANNE MOREAU

BORN IN PARIS, FRANCE IN 1928;
DIED IN PARIS, FRANCE IN 2017

Born in Montmartre to an English mother who was a dancer at the Folies Bergères cabaret and a French father, who owned a café, she fell in love with theatre at a very young age. She studied at the Conservatoire National d'Art Dramatique and in 1948, at the age of twenty she became the youngest full-time member of the Comédie Française's history (the equivalent of The Royal Shakespeare Company).

Orson Welles considered her "*the greatest actress in the world*". On screen, it's Louis Malle's film *Lift to the Scaffold* (1958) that revealed her true cinematic talent. He filmed her with no make-up and natural lighting only, which let her expressive face be the focal point of the drama. She became the queen of the French New Wave and an international star with François Truffaut's ménage à trois *Jules et Jim* (1961).

In 1965, Truffaut told a reporter for *Time* magazine,

"**She has all the qualities one expects in a woman, plus all those one expects in a man – without the inconveniences of either**."

Louis Malle, François Truffaut, Antonioni, Luis Buñuel, Peter Brook, Orson Welles... Jeanne Moreau worked with most of the greatest directors of the 1950s and 1960s. She also directed three films and was a singer/songwriter. A free spirit, a feminist living scandalous affairs, Ms Moreau was often labelled as 'femme fatale' and 'sex symbol'. She was nicknamed 'The French Bette Davis' but admitted to a journalist once that she hated that comparison! Jeanne Moreau was notorious for her strong personality, heavy smoker's husky voice, and passionately sensual nature. She once said that her soul would "burn" until the end. She is the only French actress to have had a major retrospective of her work (including 30 films) at the Museum of Modern Art in New York (in February-March 1994).

Ms Moreau loved nature and spending time in her house in the countryside. She had a special connection with cats, which was particularly visible in her role as Maggie "The Cat" in Tennessee Williams' *Cat on a Hot Tin Roof*, directed by Peter Brook (1956).

Once interviewed by Marguerite Duras, she said:

"*The love I feel in my life, the tribulations, the happiness, all of it is in the movies I've played in, all of it is intertwined in them...When I watch a film after I've been shot in it, I recognise my life in it.*"

"*I'm pleased I can be outrageous as only the English can be.*"

JULIA CHILD

BORN IN CALIFORNIA, USA IN 1912;
DIED IN CALIFORNIA, USA IN 2004

Julia Child was the first celebrity chef in America, with her cooking show The French Chef airing from 1963 to 1973.

It all started with Paris, Le Cordon Bleu and a very special companion named Minette. Julia and Paul Child moved to Paris after World War II in 1948. They had met at the former CIA, the Office of Strategic Services (OSS) where Julia was keeping intelligence files for OSS India. As a child, Julia had wanted to become a spy and was looking for adventure. One could say that she eventually unlocked the secrets of French cooking to Americans, but definitely not under cover. After enrolling at one of the oldest and most prestigious cooking schools Le Cordon Bleu, Julia embarked on a twelve-year expedition, co-writing *Mastering the Art of French Cooking* with Simone Beck and Louisette Bertholle. The book was published in 1961, a runaway bestseller paving the way for Julia's television career.

Minette was the name of the cat Julia and Paul adopted during their time in Paris. It became Julia's close companion, in the kitchen and by the dinner table. Le Cordon Bleu was a school dominated by men and Julia had to work long hours to train and prove herself. Her little Minette mascot was undoubtedly instrumental to her success. Julia once said:

"A house without a cat is like a day without sunshine, a pie without fromage, a dinner without wine."

Julia Child revolutionised American food culture as the most unlikely middle-aged television star. Her TV show was shot in one long take with very few edits, which gave a sense of live performance with its mishaps and failures. The result was spontaneous, charming, un-intimidating, with a touch of irresistible charisma.

Her autobiography *My Life in France* inspired half of the story of the film *Julie & Julia* (2009) by Nora Ephron, starring Meryl Streep as Julia Child.

Julia was also fully recognised as a cat lady in the book *Julia's Cats: Julia Child's Life in the Company of Cats*.

MERCI MINETTE!

#CHILDLESSCATLADY

IMPORTANT FACTS ABOUT JULIA

She became a celebrity chef at the age of 50

Mastering the Art of French Cooking has sold 2.5 million copies. She won a National Book Award in 1980

The French Chef cooking show won her a Peabody Award (1964) and an Emmy Award (1966)

She received French Legion of Honor in 2000 and the Presidential Medal of Freedom in 2003

Her kitchen and some of her iconic implements were put on display at the Smithsonian Institution in Washington, D.C

KAMALA HARRIS

BORN IN CALIFORNIA, USA IN 1964

"On January 20, 2021, Kamala Harris was sworn in as the 49th Vice President of the United States — the first woman, the first Black American, and the first South Asian American to be elected to this position."

HTTPS://KAMALAHARRIS.COM/ABOUT/

In August 2024, Harris was officially named the Democratic Party's presidential nominee following the withdrawal of Joe Biden from the race to the presidential election.

When Donald Trump chose JD Vance as Vice President in the run-up to the 2024 presidential election, Vance's infamous slur against Kamala Harris as another 'childless cat lady' came back to the fore on social media, sparking memes and women commenting "Never been more proud to be a childless cat lady!"

'a bunch of childless cat ladies who are miserable at their own lives and the choices that they've made and so they want to make the rest of the country miserable too'

JD Vance

In this televised interview on Fox News in 2021, he named Vice President Kamala Harris, Secretary of Transportation Pete Buttigieg and the young New York Representative Alexandria Ocasio-Cortez as politicians who had no stake in the future of America.

In summer 2024, as a reaction to this statement, female supporters of Kamala Harris set a tone of feline defiance online. Christine Pelosi, Nancy Pelosi's daughter, organised a set of Zoom calls with self-proclaimed 'cat ladies' in support of Kamala Harris' presidential campaign. Nancy Pelosi made a surprise appearance, showing support for women's freedom to"love how they wanna love and live how they wanna live."

The Democratic presidential campaign used the 'cat ladies' new popularity with a video montage on social media showing several pics of Harris' running mate Governor Tim Walz's rescue cat, Afton, and the "purr-fect" caption, "Cat people for Harris-Walz."

Whether Kamala Harris/ 'Momala' (as her two stepchildren call her) owns a cat remains unclear. And regardless, this "childless cat lady" label couldn't hold a better champion with a self-made woman like Kamala.

She is no stranger to animal rights and animal welfare support. During her 2016 US Senate campaign, one of her platform pledges was

"FIGHT FOR NATIONWIDE PROTECTIONS FOR ANIMAL RIGHTS."

"MY MOTHER WOULD OFTEN SAY TO ME: 'KAMALA, YOU MAY BE THE FIRST TO DO MANY THINGS. MAKE SURE YOU ARE NOT THE LAST'"

LAUREN BACALL

BORN IN NEW YORK, USA IN 1924;
DIED IN NEW YORK, USA IN 2014

Born Betty Joan Perske to Natalie (Weinstein) Perske and William Perske. Her father was an alcoholic and left the family when Betty was only six years old.

Betty dreamed of becoming an actress and would go see shows on Broadway as often as she could.

She was discovered by Nancy Hawks, who saw her on the cover of *Harper's Bazaar* when she started out as a model. Howard Hawks then casted her for the lead role with Humphrey Bogart in *To Have and Have Not*, in 1944. He had been looking for a different kind of star, "a woman with a masculine approach, insolent, someone who could give as good as she got". The movie was received with rave reviews and Lauren Bacall became 'The Look'. She later explained that her iconic pose, looking up with her chin down, was the only way she had found to keep her head still, as she was battling with her nerves.

The movie's promotional posters read "Slinky! Sultry! Sensational!"

Lauren Bacall and Humphrey Bogart fell in love on set and married in 1945. Her beauty and talent had struck Hollywood, and she had become a star overnight. Her deep, husky voice set her apart. Bogart would describe her as "steel with curves."

Bogart died prematurely in 1957, but they had a series of films together before then, notably *Key Largo* (in which she was called "a Wild Cat" by one of the main characters). Her career continued to grow after Bogart's death and she reinvented herself in the musical theatre world at the age of forty. She starred in more than sixty films and won two Tony Awards. She also won a National Book Award for her autobiography *By Myself* in 1979, a Lifetime Achievement Award at the Stockholm Film Festival, and an honorary Oscar in 2009.

She was a lover of animals, particularly cats, all her life. She had a beloved black cat named Blinky.

She had great affection for cats, which brings warmth and a softer touch to her distant and enigmatic persona.

She was a great admirer of their independence and once said:

"Cats are unique. They're mysterious, self-sufficient, and incredibly beautiful. They have character, and they keep you humble."

LI QINGZHAO

BORN IN JINAN, SHANDONG PROVINCE, CHINA IN 1084; DIED IN JINHUA, ZHEJIANG PROVINCE, IN 1155

IN CHINESE MYTHOLOGY, THE CAT GODDESS LI SHOU HOLDS AN IMPORTANT ROLE.

When the gods created the world, they appointed Li Shou to run the day-to-day with her fellow cats and gave them the power of speech to give orders to other creatures. On each of the creator gods' visits however, they found cats chasing a butterfly or basking in sunlight.

When questioned about the cats dedication to their task, Cat Goddess Li Shou answered:

"To be perfectly honest, we've realized that we really don't want the bother of running a world. We've noticed that one of your creatures shows much more promise in this respect, perhaps you could give the task of running a world to them so that we can spend our time enjoying the pleasures this world has to offer."

Those creatures were humans. The creator gods agreed on the sole condition that cats would no longer have the power of speech, which would be handed over to humans instead.

Cats continued to fascinate in Chinese culture, especially during the Song Dynasty, often called the 'Golden Age' of cats.

> *'Spring chill fills the upper rooms,*
>
> *For days on end the curtains are drawn on all sides:*
>
> *I am too languid to lean over the balustrade.*
>
> *The incense burnt out, my quilts feel cold*
>
> *As I wake from a new dream.'*

Extract from Li Qingzhao's poem 'The Charm of a Maiden Singer – Spring Thoughts'

The greatest woman poet in Chinese history Li Qingzhao, associated her poetry with cats and art, especially in light of nature and domestic life being the prime subjects of art and literature during the Song Dynasty.

She wrote seven volumes of essays and six volumes of poetry. Most of her work is lost except for some poetry fragments, which translate into *The Magpie at Night*. The latter is still published and described as 'iconoclastic verse', showcasing 'her visionary portrait of the inner workings of the artist's mind'.

Li Qingzhao wrote primarily ci poetry, a song form. Her mastery of the metrical rules of the form was such that she produced one of the earliest known scholarly studies of ci.

Li was raised in a literary family and her poetic talents developed at an early age. She was also known to be headstrong and fiercely competitive. Her poems boldly criticised the emperor and his favouritism towards An Lushan, which empowered him to rebel.

She had to flee Qingzhao because of the Jurchen invasion of 1125. Her poems are celebrated for their personal and emotional intensity. The death of her husband was at the origin of profound, grief-stricken poems. After nearly thirty years of marriage, Li Qingzhao did not give birth to any children...

#CHILDLESSCATLADY

MAGDALEINE PINCELOUP DE LA GRANGE, NÉE DE PARSEVAL

PAINTING BY JEAN-BAPTISTE PERRONNEAU, FRANCE 1747

In Western art history, Magdaleine Pinceloup de la Grange is known to be one of the first high society ladies to have her portraitists done with her cat. Jean-Baptiste Perronneau, one of the most prominent French portraitist at the time, painted her and her husband Charles-François Pinceloup de la Grange, separately.

Jean-Baptiste Perronneau specialised in portraits in which one could access the psychology of the sitter. He frequently painted his society subjects with feline companions to accentuate their sophistication.

Magdaleine Pinceloup de la Grange was a French aristocrat in the 18th century, and it is understood that her husband, who had received several prestigious government appointments, was also a patron of the painter Jean-Baptiste Perronneau.

This portrait of Magdaleine Pinceloup de la Grange with her cat was created within the cultural context of the Enlightenment, where ideas of human selfhood and society were central; how one wishes to be seen by society...

In 1749, the French scientist Buffon published the pioneering book in national history science, *Histoire Naturelle*, which described the life of animals and plants. We could perhaps qualify his description of cats with what we call the 'male gaze' today.

Since medieval times, cats were perceived as the accomplices of the devil and traditional companions to women who were considered 'witches' (women who didn't conform to society, often single women). Buffon was still influenced by this cultural heritage, and attributed an "innate malice" ("une malice innée") to cats, and a somewhat libertine attitude.

"The form and temperament of the cat's body perfectly correspond with his disposition. He is handsome, light, adroit, cleanly, and voluptuous; he loves ease, and searches out the softest places for rest and repose. The cat is very amorous, and what is uncommon among animals, the female appears more ardent than the male; she seeks for and invites him, and by her loud cries announces the fury of her desires or rather the pressure of her wants; if he flies from or disdains her, she pursues, tears, and though their approaches are always accompanied with acute pain, she forces him to comply with her desires"

Extracts from Buffon's *Histoire Naturelle*

In this intellectual and social context, one wonders about the multiple interpretations of Magdaleine Pinceloup de la Grange's portrait with her cat. Its Chartreux blue-gray fur mirrors the blue silk of Magadaleine's dress and the blue ribbons in her hair. Notably, in the portrait they both look away and up, perhaps a symbol of resistance and defiance. However, they both wear a collar, a symbol of domesticity for the cat and perhaps one for lady Magdaleine, whose independence might well have been limited to her relationship with her cat?

MARGHERITA HACK

BORN IN FLORENCE, ITALY IN 1922;
DIED IN TRIESTE, ITALY IN 2013

She was nicknamed 'The Lady of the Stars' ('L'amica delle stelle'). She is one of the most well-known astrophysicists of the 20th century and the first woman in Italy to become the Director of the Astronomical Observatory. In 1964, she obtained the chair of Astrophysics at the University of Trieste, which she turned from a small provincial institute to a vibrant international centre for research. Asteroid 8558 Hack is named after her. She remains a role model for women in science.

It is thought that much of Margherita's originality and progressiveness in her scientific and managerial thinking may have taken its roots from her unconventional family. She was a single child and grew up with a working mum and a stay-at-home dad. They were vegetarians because of their respect for animals, which was rare in the early 20th century in Italy! Her parents belonged to the 'Società Teosofica Italiana', an organisation which put forward Humanity as its main principle, over all religions. Margherita was an atheist and continued to believe that spirituality was to love and understand others.

Before the existence of satellites, Hack explored the universe through ultraviolet rays: "Looking at it in ultraviolet rays means being able to observe phenomena otherwise invisible" wrote the astrophysicist.

Hack specialised in researching the constant evolution of the universe and her treatise *Stellar Spectroscopy* co-written with Otto Struve, is still considered a fundamental text.

SHE WAS A BRILLIANT COMMUNICATOR, BRINGING COMPLEX CONCEPTS INTO SIMPLE LANGUAGE. SHE WAS REGULARLY ON TV AND WROTE BOOKS FOR CHILDREN.

Margherita was also well known as a 'gattara' ('cat lady' in Italian). Aside astrophysics, her other passion was cats. She had more than twenty at home. She found her first rescue cat in the street at eleven years old. She couldn't help but rescue cats as she came across them! She co-founded 'Il Gattile', an organisation in Trieste that provides shelters for rescue cats.

FUN FACTS:

Margherita Hack was born in Florence on Via Centostelle ('One hundred stars' street)

Margherita loved observing the stars through her telescope at home, with a cat resting on her lap.

French astronomer Jérôme Lalande, a cat lover, created in 1799 the Felis constellation because he wanted cats to be part of the officially recognised constellations. He placed it between Antlia and Hydra (Felis is Latin for cat).

"Gli animali si fidano di noi con piena fiducia come bambini, quindi dobbiamo rispettarli."

("Pets trust us completely, just like children do, therefore we are to respect them.")

MARIANNE FAITHFULL

**BORN IN LONDON, UK IN 1946;
DIED IN LONDON, UK IN 2025**

MARIANNE FAITHFULL HAD SEVERAL CAT LIVES WITHIN HER LIFETIME. SHE WAS FIRST KNOWN AS A 1960S SWINGING LONDON ICON, WITH HER MELANCHOLIC BALLADS AND SCANDALOUS SEX, DRUGS AND ROCK & ROLL LIFESTYLE WITH THE ROLLING STONES.

The Stones manager Andrew Loog Oldham, who launched her singing career, famously described her as

"an angel with big tits"

She once said in an interview:

"I was just cheesecake really, terribly depressing"

Marianne had an unconventional childhood, daughter of an eccentric father, an ex-MI6 agent, who led an upmarket commune where Marianne spent her early childhood. Her mother, Baroness Eva Sacher-Masoch, a Hungarian, half-Jewish former ballet dancer who had fled the Nazis in World War II, divorced her father and took Marianne, who was 6 years old then, to Reading. Marianne once said that she was raised like "one of her mother's cats". Marianne was already singing in school performances and coffee houses in Reading, when she was spotted by Andrew Loog Oldham. She was 17 when *As Tears Go By* became number one in the charts. Newspaper headlines read "Pop goes the folk sound".

She had become Mick Jagger's muse and started to make scandalous headlines. Her song "Sister Morphine" was pulled out of shops a few days after its release, considered as a 'pro drug' song. Dark

years of heroin addiction and alcoholism followed, where destitute and homeless Marianne found shelter in a bombed building of the Soho streets in London.

She rose from the ashes in 1979 with her album *Broken English*, in a scarred, husky voice, with a post-punk, new wave, raw dance sound. It became an underground hit.

"In the past I did what people told me – I tried to suss out what they wanted and gave it to them. I did this record for myself."

Unsurprisingly, "Sister Morphine" had been released on the Rolling Stones' *Sticky Fingers* (1971) album without the batting of an eyelid. Marianne took them to court later on to get her name in the credits of the song, which she had co-written with them.

She did collaborations with up-and-coming artists in the early 2000s and continued to create until the end of her life.

Marianne had a great fondness for cats and owned several throughout her life. John 'Hoppy' Hopkins took an iconic shot of her with a kitten in the sixties, that she posted on her official Facebook page in 2023 for International Cat Day. Marianne did several iconic photo shoots in the 1960s with kittens.

MARIE-ANTOINETTE

BORN IN VIENNA, AUSTRIA IN 1755;
DIED IN PARIS, FRANCE IN 1793

Marie-Antoinette's tragic story keeps fascinating the collective subconscious, as a symbol of the fallen opulence and extravagance of regal Versailles.

She was just fourteen years old when her marriage with Louis XVI was arranged by her mother the Austrian Empress, and the French Monarch Louis XV as the ultimate alliance against Prussia.

She was sent away from Vienna with fifty-seven coaches, to marry the future king of France. On arrival at the border, her 'welcoming' French escort immediately removed her sweet pug from her, as well as all personal belongings that could cause a distraction from the more serious matters awaiting her in Versailles. Marie-Antoinette was soon to discover that the etiquettes of the Palais de Versailles were rigid and full of intrigue, a gilded playground for the aristocrats, where the queen was not to engage with political affairs of the kingdom.

Marie-Antoinette's mother, the Austrian Empress, said about her daughters:

"They were born to obey and need to learn to do so in due course"

Marie-Antoinette became Queen of France at the age of seventeen. Despite all the criticism for being 'the Austrian', she became notorious for her graceful gait, radiant smile, dignified posture and the immense kindness and affection she had for children and animals. Sofia Coppola's film Marie-Antoinette (2006) celebrates her frivolity and extravagant parties. Indeed, she loved amusement more than intellectual pursuits, but it was also an escape from an unhappy life.

The infamous statement 'Let them eat cake' was historically manufactured. Such false words had wrongly been attributed to other queens and princesses before her.

When she was given the opportunity to flee besieged Versailles on the 5th of October 1789, she heroically refused; "if Parisians come to assassinate me; I will be there dying at the King's feet." Her dignity and bravery during her trial and guillotine execution were admired by her contemporaries and historians.

Despite the legend Marie-Antoinette has become, it is less known that her legacy might lie in... the Maine Coon breed in America!

THE MAINE COON: MARIE-ANTOINETTE'S GIFT TO AMERICA

While the royal family made an unsuccessful attempt at fleeing the Revolution, their belongings were sent on a ship to North America, including Marie-Antoinette's beloved Turkish Angora cats. On these new shores, it is believed that they bred with local short-haired cats, giving birth to the new breed of the Maine Coon. They are known to be large and gentle, with a stunning appearance, resilient with thick fur, tufted ears and a bushy tail, with excellent hunting skills. It is one of the oldest natural breeds in North America.

IN 1895 A MAINE COON NAMED COSY WON THE FIRST AMERICAN CAT SHOW IN MADISON SQUARE GARDENS

MARLENE DIETRICH

**BORN IN BERLIN, GERMANY IN 1901;
DIED IN PARIS, FRANCE IN 1992**

AT SEVEN YEARS OLD, MARLENE DIETRICH ALREADY INVENTED HER CHARACTER 'MARLENE' IN HER LITTLE DIARIES.

At the age of twenty, she started her career as a singer in the Berlin cabaret scene of the roaring twenties. She was spotted by the Hollywood movie director, Josef von Sternberg, who was auditioning for his next film. He launched Marlene's career as an icon of the golden age of Hollywood, where she was signed by Paramount Pictures, who wanted her to rival with MGM's Greta Garbo. Sternberg directed seven movies with Marlene Dietrich, the first one being *The Blue Angel* (1930).

STERNBERG IS KNOWN TO HAVE SHAPED MARLENE'S STAR IMAGE, WITH HIS MASTERY OF CINEMATOGRAPHY.

Marlene learnt enormously from him and would later redirect the lighting on sets herself if she were unhappy with it.

Before Audrey Hepburn and Anita Ekberg, Marlene Dietrich embodied the ultimate 'Cat Lady on Screen' in *Dishonored* (1931). Blackie, the black cat in the film, has one of the most important roles. Marlene's character is holding him close to her chest in a lot of the shots in her apartment. Blackie was initially a stray, who had wandered onto the property of Animal Land, an establishment that raised animals for film productions in Hollywood. Eventually, he became Marlene's pet.

MARLENE DIETRICH WAS OFTEN SAID TO HAVE HAD DUALITY.

Throughout her unconventional life (she was married but had many lovers), she lived short romances with men and women. She didn't want to marry again. Although she engaged in a more serious relationship with French actor Jean Gabin, she refused to settle down with him. Marlene was also known for her androgynous looks as well as ultra feminine ones. She had become a style icon, and Pierre Cardin designed her dresses for her musical shows in her later career. She was eternal glamour and elegance.

During World War II, she served in the army as an artist. She would relentlessly visit troops on the battle fronts at her own peril. She was the first non-Jewish German woman to openly oppose the Nazis and their fascist regime. She received the Presidential Medal of Freedom in 1947.

Her close circle would qualify her as a woman of duty and hard work. In an interview, her grandson said that she did 65 shows a year between the age of 65 and 72!

Marlene Dietrich was an independent woman, taking control of her life as a star, against the studio system. She was the first actress to earn shares on the profits of her films, before Clark Gable, John Wayne...

MARTHA STEWART

BORN IN NEW JERSEY, USA IN 1941

"CURIOUS", "INNOVATIVE", "BOUNDARY-BREAKING SPIRIT" ARE THE WORDS THAT DEFINE MARTHA STEWART ON HER WEBSITE.

"It's our mission to teach and inspire you to design the life you want." In other words, an ode to freedom expressed through personal choice of lifestyle and how to perfect it.

Best-selling author of 99 lifestyle books

Emmy Award-winning television show host

The show *Entertaining by Martha Stewart* was created in 1982

Founded the first multi-channel lifestyle company, Martha Stewart Living Omnimedia

The American lifestyle and cookery entertainment queen loves her animals and has been known to throw birthday parties for her Himalayan cats Verdi and Vivaldi with organic cat food cup cakes.

Martha Stewart had 6 Himalayan cats, who were brothers. She named them after great classical composers: Mozart, Beethoven, Vivaldi, Verdi, Berlioz and Bartok. Bartok, who was the last one to pass, died in 2016 at nineteen years of age. Before he did, Martha also acquired calico Persians, Princess Peony and Empress Tang. New cats and kittens have joined Martha's farm since, with her latest acquisitions being Cinco and Mayo. Cinco is a calico and Mayo a tabby. "And don't forget Blackie, my greenhouse cat. He is also doing excellently. He guards my gardens and loves greeting everyone who visits", she wrote in a November 2024 blog entry.

A RECAP OF MARTHA'S CAT BREEDS

Himalayan cats (short for Himalayan Persian, or Colourpoint Persian as it is commonly referred to in Europe), are a breed or sub-breed of long-haired cats similar in type to the Persian, with the exception of its blue eyes and its point colouration, which were derived from crossing the Persian with the Siamese.

Persian cats trace their origins to the deserts of Persia and Iran. The Persian cat is a medium to large-sized breed, easily identifiable by their round, flat face and long flowing coat that comes in almost every colour. Persian cats are gentle, loving companions even if their face makes them look a little grumpy.

Calico cats have tricolour coats. The calico cat is commonly 25 to 75% white with large orange and black patches. Calicos are almost exclusively female.

Tabby cats have a distinctive coat pattern and an "M"-shaped marking on the forehead. The pattern can include stripes, dots, lines, flecks, bands, or swirls on the cat's body, and the cat may also have stripes by its eyes and across its cheeks, back, legs, and tail

"As with all my new pets, I gently bit each kitten on the face. This is how I let my animals know that I am now their mother."

MAYUMI INABA

BORN IN AICHI, JAPAN IN 1950; DIED IN TOKYO, JAPAN IN 2014

MAYUMI INABA WAS A PRIZE-WINNING JAPANESE NOVELIST AND POET; KNOWN FOR HER SUBTLE RENDITION OF THE NATURAL WORLD AND HER SOLITARY LIFE AS AN INDEPENDENT WOMAN WRITER.

She made her debut in 1973 with the short story *The Pain of Blue Shadows* and has written two dozen novels and collections of poetry and essays. She is also known for the script of the movie *Endless Waltz* (1995), a biopic of Kaoru Abe, a Japanese free jazz/improvisation saxophonist, directed by Koji Wakamatsu.

One of her award-winning short stories narrates the story of a Tokyo librarian who mistakenly receives a call intended for a phone sex line.

The memoir of her life alongside her cat Mii is a Japanese modern classic, *Mornings Without Mii*. It was finally translated and published in the US in March 2025. The publisher describes it as "a deeply affecting story of solitude, independence, writing, grief, love, and life alongside a cat."

"A gentle meditative narrative... Inaba muses on her own life... and has to confront mortality... Cat lovers, prepare to weep'

The Times,
"Book of the Month"

Mornings Without Mii is the original title, which the US publisher kept. The UK publisher changed the title to *Mornings With My Cat Mii*. Written in 1999, it relates the twenty-year relationship of Mayumi Inaba with her cat Mii.

'She was a calico, with white, black, and tan stripes on her head and patches on her back, and a belly that was pure white.'

Mayumi Inaba,
Mornings Without Mii

The twenty-year relationship lasts longer than her marriage, the several jobs she had (she mainly worked as an editor) and the homes she lived in. Mii's declining health lays the ground for a unique and subtle relationship with Mayumi, who massages her daily, when she gets closer and closer to death. Throughout the book Mayumi describes her life keeping it close to its raw realities, kicking her husband out, getting drunk and writing with Mii lying at her feet.

Mii had become Mayumi's companion and muse at the same time. The novel is interspersed with poems and conveys a beautiful positive energy.

LITERARY AWARDS

Women's Literature Prize (1992)

The Hirabayashi Taiko Prize (1995)

The Yasunari Kawabata *Prize for Miru (The Sea Staghorn)* in 2008

The Tanizaki Jun'ichirō Prize for her memoir Hantō-e (To the Peninsula) in 2011

"As the long, long years passed, I was crawling out of a dark tunnel. The days I had spent without knowing what I wanted to write had nurtured me without my realising it. It had all started with a kitten."

NEFERTITI

BORN IN THEBES, EGYPT, C.1370 BC;
DIED IN EGYPT, C.1330 BC

Her life-size, magnificent limestone and stucco bust
was found in 1912 by the German Egyptologist Ludwig Borchardt.
It is exhibited in the Ägyptisches Museum in Berlin,
although the German ownership is heavily contested
by the Egyptian government.

Nefertiti was the wife of Pharaoh Akhenaten, who ruled in the 14th century B.C.E. and became a Pharaoh herself. Nevertheless, most facts of her exceptional life as a queen remain unknown. Her tomb is yet to be discovered.

Nefertiti gained a divine status when her husband Pharaoh Akhenaten broke away from the Ancient Egyptian polytheist religion, to create the first monotheist religion, worshipping the sun god known as the Aten. Nefertiti as well as Akhenaten were revolutionary figures of their time. They built a new city of worship to Aten, the city of Tell El-Amarna. Four years after the death of Akhenaton, the throne got back to the city of Thebes and Tell El-Amarna was abandoned.

Tutankhamun, commonly known as King Tut, was the son of Akhenaten and another wife. Nefertiti was his stepmother. Tutankhamun married his half-sister, Ankhesenamun, who was Nefertiti's daughter. Egyptologists now believe that Nefertiti's tomb could be in the same site as King Tut's tomb in the Valley of the Kings.

A family altar, exhibited in the collection of the Ägyptisches Museum in Berlin, depicts the royal couple with their three eldest daughters. It illustrates ostensibly the harmonious life of the royal family, with the protective rays of Aten. It also appears as a beautiful tribute to Nefertiti's status. She is depicted at the same scale as her husband; her name is given equal status with that of Akhenaten and the god Aten in the royal cartouche.

LEGEND HAS IT THAT NEFERTITI WAS BURIED WITH 500 CATS... THIS IS YET TO BE VERIFIED, BUT ALTHOUGH NEFERTITI AND AKHENATEN BROKE AWAY FROM ANCIENT EGYPT'S MULTIPLE DIVINITIES, CATS REMAINED AS ASSOCIATED TO THE SUN IN ANCIENT EGYPT CULTURE.

Cats were revered and held in divine status. In Egyptian mythology, Goddess Bastet was a feline-headed slender woman and considered to be a daughter of the sun. She had the dual nature of the sun's destructive fire as well as its soothing warmth when pacified. Bastet was the goddess of protection, pleasure, and the bringer of good health. Cats were sacred in Ancient Egypt.

Nefertiti undoubtedly inherited and embodied that dual nature, so commonly associated with cats in Ancient Egyptian culture, both exceptionally beautiful and powerful. Loyal to previous cat divinities, her life and death remain largely mysterious.

HER NAME TRANSLATES AS
'A BEAUTIFUL WOMAN HAS COME.'

ROSA LUXEMBURG

BORN IN POLAND, IN 1871;
DIED IN GERMANY, IN 1919

"Freedom is always, and exclusively, freedom for the one who thinks differently."

Rosa Luxemburg grew up as the youngest in a Polish and Jewish, bourgeois family. She witnessed the atrocity of the pogrom in Warsaw at a young age, in 1881. In 1889, she moved on her own to Zurich in Switzerland, home to radical Russian and Polish leftists. She was exceptionally intelligent and was one of the very few women of the time who obtained a Doctorate in Political Economy. She spoke fluent Russian, German, Yiddish, Polish and French. Although she already had a lover, the actor Leo Jogiches, she proceeded with a sham marriage to move to Berlin in Germany and start her political career.

"I am and want to remain an idealist"

she wrote in a letter to Leo early in her career

"It is only by accident that I am whirling in the maelstrom of history"

Rosa Luxemburg didn't believe in nationalism but global change instead and became one of the most prominent figures of the Left in Europe.

Her letters to her lover Leo, with whom the relationship was tumultuous, reveal how insecure she could be at times on an emotional level, and how much she longed for domestic bliss, with her beloved cat Mimi. She suffered from stress, overwork, depression, the guilt of focusing on her career and not having children... a very contemporary cat lady in fact.

Although she was an immense political influencer, hailed as highly charismatic, and keeping a correspondence with Lenin, her pacifist approach to the socialist revolution set her apart from the rest of the prominent socialists.

She believed in the power of the 'Mass Strike' and, whilst in prison, created a new movement 'The Spartacist League.' Together with the co-founder of the movement, she was tragically assassinated in 1919.

IMPORTANT FACTS ABOUT ROSA LUXEMBURG

In 1898, she published her first pamphlet *Social Reform or Revolution?*

Her pamphlet *Leninism or Marxism?* was published in 1904

Sentenced to prison for 12 months in 1915, being almost the only one among the leadership of the Social Democratic Party in Germany to oppose herself publicly to the war

She wrote *The Crisis of Social Democracy* whilst in prison. It was published in Switzerland and the text was radically anti-war

A BADASS CHILDLESS CAT LADY

Ahead of her time

A passionate activist

A bourgeois turned revolutionist

A pacifist

A feminist (she demanded equality of the sexes and sided with the great German feminist Clara Zetkin)

DOESN'T SHE EMBODY THE INDEPENDENT, DEFIANT AND DETERMINED CAT LADY IN ALL HER GLORY?

#CHILDLESSCATLADY

SADE

BORN IN IBADAN, NIGERIA IN 1959

ICONIC BRITISH BAND FROM THE 1980S, COMPOSED OF 4 MUSICIANS: LEAD SINGER AND SONGWRITER EPONYMOUS SADE, SAXOPHONIST STUART MATTHEWMAN, KEYBOARD PLAYER ANDREW HALE, AND BASSIST PAUL SPENCER DENMAN.

Born Helen Folasade Adu in Nigeria, her British mother separated from her Nigerian father when she was only 4 years old and moved to the countryside in Essex, England. Sade is a shortened form of her Yoruba middle name, Folasade, which means 'Rule with nobility'.

Sade was brought up in a house without instruments but when she spent time with her father, they would listen to a lot of jazz music together. As a teenager, she saw the Jackson 5 in a concert venue in London, "I was more fascinated by the audience than by anything that was going on on the stage. They'd attracted kids, mothers with children, old people, white, black. I was really moved. That's the audience I've always aimed for."

Her songs are centred on love and her values stand up to her Yoruba name; she rules with noble values, togetherness and loyalty. She accepted to be signed by Epic records on the condition that her bandmates would be signed too. That was refused at first. She turned them away, but they came back eventually. In addition, she insisted on a four-way split for the band, with no advantage to her as the lead.

THROUGHOUT HER CAREER, SADE HAS KEPT AS MYSTERIOUS AS HER CATS. LIVING A PRIVATE LIFE, SHE HAS GIVEN FEW INTERVIEWS AND MADE A POINT IN LIVING AS AN ARTIST AND NOT A CELEBRITY.

Consequently, each new album has been a highly anticipated event for her fanbase, which she has managed to keep close and alive for 30 years with minimum interaction and marketing.

IMPORTANT FACTS ABOUT SADE

First single "Your Love Is King" became a top 10 British hit in February 1984

First album *Diamond Life* (1984) sold more than 10 million copies worldwide

Sade's 6 albums have sold close to 40 million copies worldwide

6 multi-platinum albums released in 25 years

4 Grammy Awards including Best New Artist (1986)

Sade the artist was awarded an OBE (Officer of the Order of the British Empire) in 2002, for her contributions to music

Sade the artist was promoted to CBE (Commander of the Order of the British Empire) in 2018

"I only make records when I feel I have something to say. I'm not interested in releasing music just for the sake of selling something. Sade is not a brand."

Her latest release was a single called "Young Lion" for a benefit album, celebrating her transgender son.

Women and cats will do as they please, and men and dogs should relax and get used to the idea.

SOPHIE MARCEAU

BORN IN PARIS, FRANCE IN 1966

Sophie Marceau is a French actress, icon of our times and fierce defender of animal rights.

Sophie Marceau became a star at the young age of thirteen years old in the French film *La Boum* (*The Party*) in 1980, where falling in love for the first time is notoriously captured at a house party in a 'slow dancing' scene with a boy... Her natural confidence blew the cast directors away in her audition. Ever since she has kept that fresh style, breaking away from all manufactured codes of the star system.

She received the French equivalent of the Oscars for Young Female Emerging Talent for her role in the *Boum* sequel, *La Boum 2* (*The Party 2*) in 1982. It was the first time this prize was ever given, and it was created in the memory of French actress Romy Schneider.

Sophie Marceau has played in fifty films so far, with some international blockbusters such as *Braveheart* in 1995 and the James Bond film *The World Is Not Enough* in 1999, where she played the Bond girl alongside Pierce Brosnan. The highly successful 2008 French film *LOL* (*Laugh Out Loud*), which narrates the strong bond between a mother and her teenage daughter, was adapted in Hollywood in 2012, with Demi Moore playing Sophie Marceau's role, and Miley Cyrus playing her daughter.

Sophie is an extremely versatile artist. She sung in an album in 1985 and directed a film *Parlez-moi d'amour* (*Speak to Me of Love*) in 2002, for which she received the Best Director's Prize in the Montreal Festival that same year. In recent years, she has written books, which have been bestsellers, recognised for their literary value.

THROUGHOUT HER LIFE, SHE HAS BEEN AN ANIMAL LOVER AND A PROUD CAT LADY.

In 1991, the French actress campaigned against the abandonment of cats and dogs at Christmas time, as an ambassador for the Society for the Protection of Animals. Two hundred dogs and more than one hundred cats were offered for adoption near the Eiffel Tower.

She has been one of the most favourite celebrities in France for decades. She is personable, always radiant with a beautiful smile. She wears her heart on her sleeve. This nature has brought her to make many blunders... for that reason, she has been the subject of recurring mockery. However, she was one of the first actresses to be vocal about some male directors and actors' inappropriate behaviour in the cinema industry.

She is a self-made actress, who has always held her head high and fought for her values.

A PROPER BADASS CONTEMPORARY CAT LADY!

TAYLOR SWIFT

BORN IN PENNSYLVANIA, USA IN 1989

"The most famous childless cat lady in the world has spoken. Taylor Swift's endorsement of Kamala Harris 'comes at a time when Swift has never been more popular, powerful, and ever-present,' as Tyler Foggatt writes."

A thread posted for the *New Yorker* 11/09/24

With the Eras Tour in 2023 and 2024, Taylor Swift became the queen supreme of the global music scene. It was the highest-grossing music tour ever, becoming the first to surpass $1 billion in revenue. She was heralded as 'Time Person of the Year' in 2023, making her the first musician ever to gain that distinction. *Time's* editor-in-chief Sam Jacobs went on to describe her as "the rare person who is both the writer and the hero of her own story", adding that she had 'found a way to transcend borders and be a source of light'.

"I will be casting my vote for Kamala Harris and Tim Walz in the 2024 Presidential Election. I'm voting for @kamalaharris because she fights for the rights and causes I believe need a warrior to champion them."

Taylor Swift, Childless Cat Lady

The *Time* magazine's cover heralding Taylor Swift's portrait was the epitome of the proud cat lady spirit, with Taylor's famous Ragdoll Benjamin Button wrapped round her neck, in a mink like fashion.

Taylor is indeed the proud mum to three cats: two Scottish Folds named Meredith Grey and Olivia Benson, and her Ragdoll Benjamin Button.

Recently, she bought back master recordings for her early repertoire, regaining control over all her music. Her most discreet cat so far, Meredith, kept her company on the video for the official announcement.

```
   /\_/\
 = ( · · ) =
   /     \
```

"I am proud of my 'childless cat lady' status. It shows that a woman can be accomplished without following traditional societal norms."

"Curious, cat lover, romantic."

Taylor Swift describing herself in 3 words

TAYLOR STARRED IN *CATS* THE MOVIE IN 2019. DURING THE SHOOT, SHE WENT EVERY DAY TO 'CAT SCHOOL' FOR FOUR MONTHS, WHERE SHE LEARNT TO CRAWL AND MOVE LIKE A CAT.

VIVIEN LEIGH

BORN IN DARJEELING, INDIA IN 1913;
DIED IN LONDON, UK IN 1967

"Once you have kept a Siamese cat you would never have any other kind. They make wonderful pets and are so intelligent they follow you around like little dogs."

Vivien Leigh, one of the 20th century's greatest actresses and one of the greatest movie stars of all time, was undeniably Cat Lady Supreme.

Vivian Mary Hartley was born in India to a wealthy British family. She was sent to boarding school in a convent in the UK when she was only 7 years old. She didn't see her mother for another 2 years. On school holidays, she would be left on her own and the Mother Superior gave her a little kitten to keep her company. She once said that she thought she was the youngest at the school and...

"so I imagine I was rather spoiled. I remember I was allowed to take cats to bed with me. I've always been mad about cats."

Vivian went to study at RADA (the Royal Academy of Dramatic Arts) and started acting. At the age of 22, she became an overnight sensation with the play *The Mask of Virtue*. She had set her eyes on Laurence Olivier, theatre genius of the time, whom she married a few years later. Vivien Leigh's defining roles came with some of America's most classic movies. She played Scarlett O'Hara in *Gone with the Wind* (1939), and Blanche DuBois in Elia Kazan's iconic adaptation of Tennessee Williams' *A Streetcar Named Desire*

(1951), with Marlon Brando. For both roles, she won the Oscar for Best Actress.

Vivien Leigh was strikingly beautiful, and her looks were often celebrated before her talent, although she was an extraordinary actress. Once asked about what theatre brought to her, she replied with a quote by George Bernard Shaw:

"a factory of thought, a prompter of conscience, an elucidator of social conduct, an armory against despair and dullness and a temple to the Ascent of Man."

In 1946, Laurence Olivier gifted his wife their first Siamese cat, a graceful feline they named New Boy - or simply New - after the New Theatre (now the Noël Coward Theatre) on St Martin's Lane in London.

Vivien went on to have several other cats, one of her favourites being Poo Jones, named after Jones Harris, a young admirer. This smoky white Siamese, marked with black and striking violet eyes, often travelled with Leigh and was known to perch on her shoulder. During stage performances, he would sleep through the acts, waking as soon as Leigh exited the stage. Poo Jones was by Vivien's side when she died, keeping vigil after she collapsed. Following her death, her housekeeper took over his care.

WHOOPI GOLDBERG

BORN IN NEW YORK, USA IN 1955

Caryn Elaine Johnson grew up in a housing estate in Manhattan, New York, and joined a youth theatre company. Dyslexic, she dropped out of high school at the age of seventeen and in 1974, moved to California where she helped found the San Diego Repertory Company. She had her comedic break with a one-woman show on a HBO special, which was the foundation for her award-winning Broadway show *Whoopi Goldberg* in 1984.

On screen, it was her role in *The Color Purple* (1985), directed by Steven Spielberg, that propelled her into stardom. Whoopi Goldberg is the first Black woman to get an EGOT: an Emmy, a Grammy, an Oscar and a Tony award.

GRAMMY: 1985 for the *Whoopi Goldberg* show's recording

OSCAR: 1991 Best Supporting Actress in *Ghost*

TONY: 2002 for producing the Broadway show *Thoroughly Modern Millie*

EMMY: 2002 for hosting the TV special *Beyond Tara: The Extraordinary Life of Hattie McDaniel*; and in 2009 for co-hosting *The View*

> After meeting Pope Francis at the Vatican, Whoopi admitted that she was jetlagged on her return home and mistook her cats' treats for pretzels.

RUSSIAN BLUE CHARACTERISTICS

Blue-grey coat

Emerald green eyes

Slender, muscular build

Intelligent and affectionate

She had the lead role in the musical comedy *Sister Act* (1992), in which she performed all the singing herself. It was a tremendous commercial success.

THROUGHOUT HER LIFE, WHOOPI GOLDBERG HAS BEEN AN ACTIVIST DEFENDING CAUSES INCLUDING PRO-CHOICE RIGHTS, AIDS RESEARCH, AND CHILDREN'S WELFARE.

Her autobiography was published in 2024 as *Bits and Pieces: My Mother, My Brother and Me*. A reviewer from *Publishers Weekly* wrote:

"This is no dishy Hollywood tell-all- it's a salve for wounded souls."

All her life, Whoopi has celebrated her cat lady life. Sadly Oliver, her Russian blue, passed away in 2021 at the age of twenty. On her daily TV show *The View*, she was used to giving regular updates about Oliver.

In 2011, a five-month-old Russian blue kitten nicknamed "Verrazano" became an internet sensation because it had been thrown from a moving car on New York City's Verrazzano-Narrows Bridge and New York City Animal Care and Control were looking for someone to adopt it. Whoopi jumped to the rescue. It came on her show, and she was completely smitten, burying her face in its belly. She later announced officially that she had adopted the cat and called him Vinny. She added that her other cat Oliver was "not too happy" about the newcomer.

Let's also remember that Whoopi Goldberg was the Cheshire Cat herself in TV movie *Alice in Wonderland* (1999).

"Scratch your Freedom"

Tilly Cat

COULD FELINE FEMINISM BE THE ANSWER TO FELINE SEXISM?

To the old sexist labels of 'Crazy Cat Lady' and 'Sex Kitten', the catchy tags 'Proud Cat Lady' and 'Childless Cat Lady' are fitting echoes reclaiming the myth.
Whether their childhood was gold or grey, these women found the strength to become trailblazers and stand up for who they were/are today.

"Cats don't let you touch them.
Cats tell you what they're going to do,
and that's that."

Gloria Steinem

LONG LIVE
FELINE FEMINISM!

PURRFECT WISDOM...

"Cats, with their punky attitudes, have taught me defiance and everything else worth knowing. They are sensualists, things of beauty, who've inspired artists for centuries. Lennon, McCartney, Bowie, Dylan and many of the greatest rock stars were all crazy-cat ladies."

–Britt Collins, bestselling author of
Strays: A Lost Cat, a Homeless Man, and Their Journey Across America

"A woman cannot survive on books alone. She also needs a cat"

Anon.

"What greater gift than the love of a cat?"

Charles Dickens

"*A house without a cat is like a day without sunshine, a pie without fromage, a dinner without wine.*"

Julia Child

"*I look at her and see the absolute perfection — the charming perfection — of her imperfection.*"

(about a snaggletoothed rescue)

Alice Walker

"*I have lived with several Zen masters – all of them cats*"

Eckhart Tolle

"*Faites des bêtises, mais faites-les avec enthousiasme.*"

('Do foolish things, but do them with enthusiasm')

Colette

LE CHAT, PAR EMILY BRONTË
('THE CAT' BY EMILY BRONTË)

MAY 15TH, 1842

'I can say with sincerity that I like cats; also I can give very good reasons why those who despise them are wrong.

A cat is an animal who has more human feelings than almost any other being. We cannot sustain a comparison with the dog, it is infinitely too good; but the cat, although it differs in some physical points, is extremely like us in disposition.

There may be people, in truth, who would say that this resemblance extends only to the most wicked men; that it is limited to their excessive hypocrisy, cruelty, and ingratitude; detestable vices in our race and equally odious in that of cats.

Without disputing the limits that those individuals set on our affinity, I answer that if hypocrisy, cruelty, and ingratitude are exclusively the domain of the wicked, that class comprises everyone. Our education develops one of those qualities in great perfection; the others flourish without nurture, and far from condemning them, we regard all three with great complacency. A cat, in its own interest, sometimes hides its misanthropy under the guise of amiable gentleness; instead of tearing what it desires from its master's hand, it approaches with a caressing air, rubs its pretty little head against him, and advances a paw whose touch is soft as down. When it has gained its end, it resumes its character of Timon; and that artfulness in it is called hypocrisy. In ourselves, we give

it another name, politeness, and he who did not use it to hide his real feelings would soon be driven from society.

"But," says some delicate lady, who has murdered a half-dozen lapdogs through pure affection, "the cat is such a cruel beast, he is not content to kill his prey, he torments it before its death; you cannot make that accusation against us." More or less, Madame. Your husband, for example, likes hunting very much, but foxes being rare on his land, he would not have the means to pursue this amusement often, it he did not manage his supplies thus: once he has run an animal to its las breath, he snatches it from the jaws of the hounds and saves it to suffer the same infliction two or three more times, ending finally in death. You yourself avoid the bloody spectacle because it wounds your weak nerves. But I have seen you embrace your child in transports, when he came to show you a beautiful butterfly crushed between his cruel fingers; and at that moment, I really wanted to have a cat, with the tail of a half-devoured rat hanging from its mouth, to present as the image, the true copy, of your angel. You could not refuse to kiss him, and it he scratches us both in revenge, so much the better. Little boys are rather liable to acknowledge their friends' caresses in that way, and the resemblance would be more perfect. They know how to value our favours at their true price, because they guess the motives that prompt us to grant them, and if those motives might sometimes be good, undoubtedly they remember always that they owe all their misery and all their evil qualities to the great ancestor of humankind. For assuredly, the cat was not wicked in Paradise.'

TILLY
BOOKS

© Danann Media Publishing Limited 2024

First published in the UK 2025 by Tilly Books an imprint of Danann Media Publishing Ltd.

CAT NO: SON0609

Illustrator: **Emily Skinner**
Author: **Tilly**
Editor: **Tilly**
Designer: **Samantha Richiardi**
Proofreader: **Sofia Della Valle**

Printed in Dubai.
ISBN: 978-1-917259-35-4

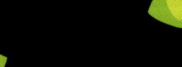
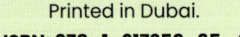